Climb Your Stairway to Heaven

Climb Your Stairway to Heaven

The 9 habits of maximum happiness

David Leonhardt

Writer's Showcase
San Jose New York Lincoln Shanghai

Climb Your Stairway to Heaven
The 9 habits of maximum happiness

Writer's Showcase
an imprint of iUniverse.com, Inc.

For information address:
iUniverse.com, Inc.
5220 S 16th, Ste. 200
Lincoln, NE 68512
www.iuniverse.com

ISBN: 0-595-17826-X

Printed in the United States of America

DEDICATION

I dedicate this book to my wife, Chantal, with whom I began this voyage of discovery. She helped me learn so much about happiness. She offered me her bottomless patience and endless support when I would spend hours on end in front of the computer screen, losing complete track of time. Together, may we continue building our Stairways to Heaven.

CONTENTS

ACKNOWLEDGEMENTS

A big *thank you* to my review panel who kept me on the right track: Michael Greene, OSP, Chantal Leonhardt, Joel Leonhardt, Aaron Leonhardt, Eve-Marie Bruneau, and Karen Hegman.

I am also grateful to the research staff at the Toronto Reference Library, who helped me access the many scientific and other sources on which this book is based.

Thank you also to iUniverse.com, who removed the formidable barriers to publishing, as well as to Theresa Danna for her invaluable proofreading.

A special thanks to my wife, Chantal, who convinced me to use my own illustrations in this work, in addition to all the help she gave me on the manuscript.

Finally, a widespread thanks to the many Toastmasters whose speeches inspired elements and anecdotes of this book.

PROLOGUE

A clumsy sheep and a silly old goat fell into an abandoned well. Her name was Sarah Sheep and his was Bray Goat, and bray he did until old Farmer Brown came. Sarah Sheep and Bray Goat were thrilled. Their old pal would save them. But the poor old farmer saw things differently. The clumsy sheep and the silly old goat were getting long in the tooth and were quite useless around the farm. And the well, which must have been a mile deep, hadn't been used in years. Besides, old Farmer Brown had no idea how to pull animals from a well.

Sarah Sheep bahhed as loudly as she could. Bray Goat kept braying, night and day, until the old farmer could take it no longer. So he started filling up the abandoned well with stones. When the stones bury the animals, he reasoned, the bahhing and braying will stop.

At first, the sheep and the goat could not believe their eyes. Stones pelted their backs. Stones hit their heads. Stones piled up around their feet. Sarah Sheep froze. Bray Goat panicked. They would surely suffocate under the growing pile of stones.

At that very moment, the small round patch of sky above was Heaven. And that gave Sarah Sheep an idea. Join Sarah Sheep and Bray Goat as they build their very own Stairway to Heaven, and learn the secrets they use to get there.

INTRODUCTION

*There are two paths you can go by, but in the long run
There's still time to change the road you're on.*

—rock band Led Zeppelin in "Stairway to Heaven"

Generations of explorers searched for it. Philosophers tried to define it. Scientists pooh-poohed it. Ordinary folk just want to know how to get there.

Heaven. The secret to happiness.

I have some good news for you and some bad news. The bad news is that there is no secret to happiness. There is no password, no secret handshake, no magic potion. There is no sage elder perched atop a mountain waiting just for you to find him and ask, "Master, what is the secret to happiness?"

The good news is that it doesn't matter—you can find happiness on your own. Actually, you can *make* happiness. You can build and climb your very own Stairway to Heaven right here on earth, and this book will help you.

Does the idea of heaven on earth mean there is no afterlife? No. I believe an afterlife exists. But we can discuss that later…like when I get there. I don't propose building a stairway to *that* heaven.

If you want to live in heaven, why wait until you die? Poet Elizabeth Browning said, "Earth's crammed with heaven." No less an authority than the Pope himself says that Heaven "is neither an abstraction nor a physical place in the clouds."

This book is not about religion, but the nine habits in this book can help you create a heaven on earth. And they may even help you find Heaven in your afterlife, too.

Heaven on earth is not absolute happiness. If I promise you that, I would be a liar. Heaven on earth is maximum happiness, the most happiness you can reach, and that I can promise you. In fact, I do. But you have to make it happen.

Not everybody gets there. You can be one of the select few who do. You can build your own unique, custom Stairway to Heaven. If you are reading this book, you clearly want to. Congratulations, you made an important decision. In the words of track athlete Jim Ryun, "Motivation is what gets you started. Habit is what keeps you going."

That's what Sarah Sheep and Bray Goat find out. Now, if you have to ask, "Who are Sarah Sheep and Bray Goat?" you did not read the prologue. I suggest you read it, because you might find parts of this book confusing if you don't.

You may rightly want to know if I found maximum happiness. The answer is: "Not yet, but I am closer than ever—and the habits in this book are bringing me closer every day." Yes, they do work; I can testify to that.

As I draft this introduction, I recall a conversation from just yesterday. My sister-in-law was yearning to return to her high school years. Those were the good old days she remembered so fondly. My brother offered a different perspective. "I'm happier than I've ever been," he said. "Each year, I keep getting happier." Upon reflection, we all agreed.

And I'm happier since I began applying the nine habits of maximum happiness. To give credit where credit is due, my wife, Chantal, and I read about five habits of very happy people in a magazine clipping a few years ago. The messages rang so true for us that we started applying all five. Over the course of two years, we discovered four more habits. So now there are nine. And we are much happier because we are applying all nine.

Why haven't we achieved maximum happiness yet? The simple answer is that habits don't change overnight. As I said earlier, there is no secret password or magic formula. Happiness takes effort. But the payback is better than winning the lottery.

Unlike many other books on happiness, *Climb Your Stairway to Heaven* gives you just nine simple habits to adopt. Not 102 tedious steps. Not 36 major life changes. Just nine simple habits to make happiness more accessible to you. Most importantly, this book will help you understand how to control your own level of happiness.

You might wonder why I would share this precious information with you. And I would love to tell you. In fact, I will. But that is part of a later chapter.

So I invite you to join me and start building your own Stairway to Heaven.

PART I

UNDERSTANDING HAPPINESS

CHAPTER 1

The Wall and your Stairway

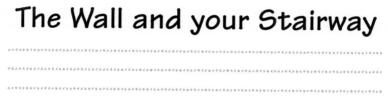

*Blame yourself if you have no branches or leaves;
don't accuse the sun of partiality.*

—Chinese proverb

You exist. That's all you really know for sure. If you ever heard tales of concentration camp survivors, you know what I mean. When stripped to the bones, we have nothing but ourselves.

Psychologist Viktor Frankl describes the desolation of a concentration camp: "We really had nothing now except our bare bodies–even minus hair; all we possessed, literally, was our naked existence." He retained only his glasses and his belt. The belt he traded for a piece of bread.

Imagine owning no shoes, no socks, no shirt, no underwear. You have just yourself.

You have yourself…but is your self happy? Most people today appear satisfied with their lives. Surprisingly, even Viktor Frankel was. Maybe you are one of the happy people. In a 1998 Gallup poll, 91 percent of Americans said they are satisfied with their family life, 86 percent with their housing and their health, 85 percent with their transportation, and 84 percent with their opportunities to succeed. Yay!

How *you* answer depends largely on your vision of happiness. Everybody wants happiness, but few people seem sure of what it is. What you get out of this book depends on how you define happiness.

Happiness researcher (honest, there is such a thing) Ed Diener, Ph.D., of the University of Illinois, lists three concepts of happiness.

1. Virtue or holiness: This is the happiness of the Greek stoics. You are happy if you possess desirable qualities. Aristotle called this "eudaimonia" or the ideal state of being.
2. Life satisfaction: This is the positive evaluation of your life. If you feel satisfied with your life, you are happy. You are content. You relax in the green pastures.
3. Pleasant emotional experience: This is how you feel at the moment–joy, fun, elation. You experience pleasure. You feel good.

Let's not quibble over definitions. Two statues stood in the city park for as long as anyone could remember. One was David, the other was Venus. One man, one woman, both naked. One day, the fairy god-mother of statues appeared, waved her wand, and **POOF!**—the statues came to life. "You have one hour before you return to stone, one hour to do what you've always wanted to do," she offered with a wink.

The statues jumped for joy and scurried off into the park. From behind a bush, the fairy godmother heard sounds of glee and physical exertion. "Oh, yes! That was wonderful," the Venus statue cried. "More, more, I want more."

"Just a minute," snapped the David statue. "It's my turn to mess up a pigeon."

What's in a name?

How appropriate that Hope College is home to one of America's foremost happiness researchers, David Myers.

The colors of happiness are different for each of us, but they usually include all of the above (the three concepts, that is, not attacks on wildlife)—what David Myers, Ph.D., another happiness researcher, calls "an enduring sense of positive wellbeing." *definition of happiness*

∞ *Welcome stonemason you* ∞

Life is hell. There are few moments of happiness.
I feel that when one experiences one of them
it is right to enjoy it. Cheers, everybody.

—English playwright Harold Pintor in a toast at his stepson's wedding

Faced with adversity, some people recite this prayer: "God, grant me the serenity to accept the things I cannot change, the courage to change the things I can, and the wisdom to know the difference." This chapter helps us develop that wisdom. After all, why try to change what is already etched in stone? We gain happiness by improving those things we can change.

The Great Wall of Misery surrounds us, a barricade between us and the Green Pastures of Cloud Nine. You might even have bumped into the Wall once or twice. **OOF**! But if we could stand atop the Wall, we would reach heaven on earth. That's where your Stairway to Heaven helps. It leads you over the Wall. You are both the climber and the stonemason. This is a self-help, do-it-yourself type book, you know.

In the chapters ahead, we'll assemble the tools you'll need—the nine habits of maximum happiness. These tools will help you move stones from the Great Wall of Misery to your Stairway to Heaven—to lower the Wall as you build up your Stairway.

The metaphor of the Wall and your Stairway helps us understand how various elements of life influence our happiness, how we can infuse our life with joy, and how we can avoid unnecessary misery. Put on your explorer's cap. It's time to inspect the Wall.

The Wall is tall. It towers above us. On closer inspection, notice the four distinct layers, each one built from stones of a different size:

Layer 1: Foundation stones so big they resemble planets

Layer 2: Habitat stones heavy enough to give a strong man a hernia

Layer 3: Barely liftable dew stones

Layer 4: Pocket-sized multiple-choice stones

Let's start climbing your Stairway to take a sneak peek at these four layers.

∞ *Layer 1: Foundation stones* ∞

There are no rules. Just follow your heart.

—comedian Robin Williams

Both the Great Wall of Misery and your Stairway to Heaven are built on a row of mighty foundation stones. Each stone weighs several tons and is as permanent as the terra firma on which it rests.

Foundation stones are your genes, your childhood, your past experiences—everything that is complete, finished, unchangeable. These stones really cannot be moved. They are part of you and your past. Now if only you had a time machine…

You might wish to move or improve some of the unhappy foundation stones. You might want to blow some to smithereens. When Ben Stevenson became artistic director of the Houston Ballet, he said, "I wanted to build the company from the bottom up." You might feel that way about your life. But if you're old enough to read this book (you are, right?), it's already too late. You can rebuild, but not from the bottom.

The Wall's very first stones are your genes. You inherited them. Your parents might spend the rest of your inheritance, but your genes are yours for keeps. Since 1924, the "nature versus nurture" debate has raged: are we more the products of nature (our genes) or nurture (our environment)?

POP QUIZ:

How much of your happiness do you control?

ANSWER: Today, most researchers say that genes determine about half of our character. That leaves the other half in your hands. Great news! The unmovable foundation stones form only half of the Great Wall of Misery.

More great news. Unlike other mammals, whose brains are 98 percent developed at birth, ours are just 38 percent developed. That leaves 62 percent for us to mold. Now that's empowerment!

Other foundation stones formed when you were young. University of Kentucky researchers put seven types of childhood trauma to the test: death of a parent or sibling, unhappily married parents, family breakup, alcohol or drug addiction in the home, emotional problems, child abuse or neglect, and serious illness. Do any of these sound familiar? They found that every one, except illness, dampens an adult's happiness. People who suffered more than one childhood trauma are even less happy and earn lower income as adults. These are Layer 1 foundation stones in the Wall—they can't be moved.

Just as some childhood experiences might have scraped you with trauma, some bathed you with warmth, love, security. Those are the foundation stones of your Stairway.

Why do I highlight the nature versus nurture debate? So you don't waste precious time struggling to change those things you cannot. This book focuses on what you can change. So let's leave the Layer 1 foundation stones alone.

✆ *Layer 2: Habitat stones* ✆

*I have the good fortune to have had a pain problem,
which has given me more insight into my patients.*

—Dr. Paul Kelly, pain specialist

Set atop the immense foundation stones are the Layer 2 habitat stones: our environment, our surroundings, our situation. Some of these we choose, some we do not. For instance, if you are born into the slums of Bangladesh, your habitat stones might be tough to move.

Most Americans choose their habitat stones, whether they know it or not. If you have the means to read this book, you control most of your habitat stones. You might relocate your career to earthquake-prone San Francisco or cultivate your hometown Iowa roots. You may study languages that could open the door to a life abroad or focus on bonding with your Missouri family.

My mother made a tough choice when she was just 17. The daughter of a prominent Budapest dentist, she was an easy target for the invading Russians. When the Communists stormed into Hungary, she sneaked out on the underground railroad. Way to go, Mom! (Please forgive my excitement. If she had not moved her habitat stones, I would never have been born.)

One person relocates from Chicago to Alaska to escape the rat race. Another moves from Alaska to Chicago to feel connected. Where do you want to go? As Napoleon Bonaparte said, "Circumstances—what circumstances? I *make* circumstances."

You can't avoid some situations: the loss of a child, a spouse, a limb. Months after his wife died, Thomas Jefferson told a friend that he had emerged from a "stupor of mind" which had rendered him "as dead to the world as she was whose loss occasioned it."

Other Layer 2 habitat stones you treasure: the forest behind your house, your fulfilling career or a caring, loving family. These are the habitat stones of your Stairway to Heaven.

Although some Layer 2 habitat stones are moveable, it takes much more than a book to guide you through that process. Let's leave the habitat stones alone…for now. You might want to revisit them once you've mastered the habits in this book.

∞ *Layer 3: Dew stones* ∞

When one door of happiness closes, another opens;
but often we look so long at the closed door
that we do not see the one which has been opened for us.

—Helen Keller

Like morning dew on the grass, you feel the Layer 3 dew stones. Some might even dampen your spirit, but they don't last. They are the events that pass through your days.

Some dew stones can be moved. You choose not to trip over something tomorrow by picking it up today. You choose not to develop food poisoning by handling raw chicken with care. You choose to enjoy this book (I hope) by reading it.

Some dew stones cannot be moved. Becky Farrar was at a loss for words. What do you say when a pumpkin crashes through your roof and smashes your kitchen table to bits? It seems two Illinois skydivers were playing a friendly little game of pass-the-big-orange-thing-around when "Oops!" Good thing nobody was sitting at the table just then.

In a less fortunate incident, Kimberly Petrella will never forget the look of horror on the subway driver's face. A man had just jumped in front of the train and smashed into it…not once, but twice. That same man seemed so serene on the bus just minutes earlier. She wished she had not witnessed that event. But the choice was not hers to make.

Although in the Great Wall of Misery they distress you, in your Stairway to Heaven the dew stones are joyous events like the really, really big hug your daughter gives you for no particular reason. Or the flowers your spouse sends you for your birthday.

Events tend to lose their impact on happiness in less than three months, and most major events no longer affect happiness after six months. The best way to deal with the dew stones is to embrace those in your Stairway while they last and just ignore those in your Wall until they fade away. Choose to be happy, step over Layer 3 of the Wall, and focus on Layer 4, where the nine habits of maximum happiness come into play.

Layer 4: Multiple-choice stones

One simple stone placed on another
is the work that builds a cathedral!

—*Good News Network* coordinator Geraldine Weis-Corbley

High up on the Wall sit the multiple-choice stones—so high they seem out of reach. They sit on the Wall, but not on the Stairway. The only way to climb your Stairway, to scale the Wall, to reach the Green Pastures of Cloud Nine is to move those Layer 4 multiple-choice stones from the Wall to your Stairway. And, you guessed it—the multiple-choice stones test you daily. They are hundreds, maybe thousands, of choices you make each day. Those choices are your reactions.

Our reactions deliver a simple verdict: happy or unhappy. An 87-year-old jazz saxophone player in New Orleans endured a stroke. Did he moan about it? No. He rejoiced that, no longer able to play the saxophone, he would finally sing with his band. He moved his stones and lowered the Great Wall of Misery.

POP QUIZ:

You're enjoying a relaxing honeymoon on a Florida beach when a pelican flies into you. How do you react?
1. Shake your fist and shout, "Watch where you're flying!"
2. Pull out a semi-automatic rifle and start a new trend: pelican rage.
3. Report the incident to the FAA and demand pelican regulations.
4. Figure this is one tale none of your friends will ever top.
ANSWER: Option four is the happy choice. Besides, have you ever *seen* how a pelican flies? Better to find a positive way to react. That's how to move the Layer 4 multiple-choice stones off the Wall.

React positively to things!

Pain is inevitable; suffering is not. Pain happens *to* us, but we choose whether we suffer from it. For years, the cover of my résumé began with a quote from Aldous Huxley: "Experience is not what happens to a man. It is what he does with what happens to him." With every year, I believe that more strongly. Keep moving those stones.

That's just what Sarah Sheep does. Remember in the Prologue how Sarah Sheep and Bray Goat were pelted with stones and how the stones are piling up around them. They could be buried alive in that old well. But Sarah Sheep is clumsy, not stupid. She shakes the stones off her back, lifts one foot at a time, and steps up onto the pile at her feet. Bray Goat follows her example, moves the stones, and stands on top of them. In their own unique way, the sheep and the goat build their Stairway to Heaven.

How do you move the multiple-choice stones? By choosing to be happy. That's the first step. Remember, they are *multiple-choice* stones. When the world deals your cards, you can choose to be happy. You can also choose to be sad. Or angry. Or frustrated. It's your choice. As British novelist Phyllis Bottome said, "There are two ways of meeting difficulties. You alter the difficulties or you alter yourself to meet them."

Remember, even if the Wall seems to tower above you and your Stairway passes for a footstool, you can build up your Stairway and lower the Wall. The Carthaginian General Hannibal sacked ancient Rome when he attacked it not by sea, as the Romans expected, but by land. Hannibal led an army of tropical elephants over the snow-covered Alps to crush Rome. As Hannibal said, "We will either find a way, or make one." Talk about scaling a wall!

Choose happiness

If you choose not to decide, you still have made a choice.

—rock band Rush in "Free Will"

Chantal burst into the room. "The dishwasher's *really* leaking now! Not just a cup of water this time, but suds, soap bubbles. We'd better call someone about it." Then, after a brief pause, "On the plus side, it gave me plenty of water and soap to wash the floor." By her reaction, she moved her stones from the Great Wall of Misery to her Stairway to Heaven. (I didn't have the heart to tell her I had washed the floor just a few hours earlier.)

Exercise:
Think about everything that affects your happiness. Write them down. To which layer in the Wall or in your Stairway does each belong? Which ones do you want to change? Which ones *can* you change?

So much happens around us, to us, at us, with us, in us, on us. Whoa! So many stones to move. So many to keep track of. How can we control them all? How can we even keep track of them all? The answer is to develop habits, so reactions that inspire happiness become second nature. And when happiness comes naturally, we can enjoy it more than when we force it.

In the chapters ahead, we will learn the nine habits of maximum happiness. But first, let's look at some of the racketeers who can sabotage our every effort to boost our happiness. In Chapter 2, we'll stand face to face with the Merchants of Misery (for we can defeat only the enemy we know).

If you don't really, really want to be happy, don't bother reading any further. Hey, this book could make a great paperweight. But if you are determined to be happy, read on.

CHAPTER 2

The Merchants of Misery

*If you make a habit of buying things you do not need,
you will soon be selling things you do.*

—Filipino proverb

Who are these Merchants of Misery? They are crafty rascals who conspire to sell us a fairy tale—the fantasy that we can sneak around the ends of the Wall. They beckon us, "Why waste time and effort moving stones when you can just walk around the Wall? The end is just out of sight." But it's just a ruse. There is no end to the Wall. There is just a treadmill the Merchants of Misery set up—a treadmill turning too fast for most people to jump off.

The Merchants of Misery work in mysterious ways. They disguise themselves as fame and wealth and goodies and approval. They masquerade as status. They hide behind the Mask of Success. Saaaayy...Success doesn't sound so bad. That's something everybody wants, right?

POP QUIZ: ....

Just what do we want?

ANSWER: A survey of American teens reveals that they want happiness more than anything—more than life, love, success, and friendship. In another survey, Canadians said they believe the world is healthier and more intelligent now, but with less happiness and worse morals than it used to have. Is this success? Just how do we measure success?

Typical measures of success are wealth and possessions, fame and status. Or more bluntly, goodies and approval. Most people strive for these all their lives, often at great cost to themselves, their families, and their own happiness. Their intentions are often well placed. After all, these are worthy goals. It's healthy to seek a comfortable home for our family, a solid education for our kids, good food on the table, and recognition for our accomplishments. On the other hand, it's healthy to eat cabbage, but don't eat five heads a day. How you measure success makes the difference between happiness and misery.

Many self-help books wear the Mask of Success: achieve results, do more in less time, get rich quick, climb the corporate ladder. The success books won't make you happy. They might help you become "successful," whatever that means, but not necessarily happy. They might even convince you to stay on the treadmill (with the end of the Wall just out of sight) instead of building your Stairway to Heaven.

Some people jump off a speeding treadmill that no longer fulfills them. Corporate lawyers become teachers. Teachers become financiers. Financiers become ministers. Ministers become Web page designers. (Okay, that's stretching it a bit.) Having achieved their career goals, they abandon their hard-earned money and status to pursue careers they now find more fulfilling. You might read about them from time to time. You might even think, "Hey, I should do that." But few of us muster the inner strength to hop off the tread-mill.

In this chapter, we'll test-drive various measures of success. Why bother, you ask? This book gives you nine habits to help you become happier, to help you move stones from the Wall to your Stairway... and to climb up on top of them. Those habits will be almost as useful as a bicycle in quicksand if the Merchants of Misery send you scurrying after the non-existent end of the Wall.

✑ *Climbing the career ladder* ✑

There are career choices and there are life choices.
That was a life choice.

—actress Michelle Pfeiffer on deciding not to star in *Evita*

The most common symbol of success is a new job or a promotion. The career ladder is where most of us receive formal recognition. A few people win contests, but almost everyone gets hired, and many people get promoted.

Unfortunately, many parents urge their children to follow a career track with "high earning potential" instead of supporting them in what they wish to do. By the time we are old enough to make decisions, many of us believe the career ladder is the only path to success.

Climbing the career ladder is not the same as climbing your Stairway to Heaven. In 1999, 93 percent of American, Canadian, and British women said they are in a better position than their grandmothers' generation. But when asked if they were happier than their grandmothers' generation, only 28 percent of Americans said, "Yes." In Canada, 33 percent agreed, as did 42 percent in Britain.

WITH GREAT DETERMINATION, WALLACE CLIMBS THE CAREER LADDER.

Women still appear to be happier than men, but American surveys show the gap is closing as women's employment and educational levels approach those of men. Career ladders seem to lead us away from happiness.

Studies show that people who order their minions around from the cell phones in their BMWs are no happier than those whose work-worn hands flip through the tabloids on the bus. Nor are they necessarily less happy.

POP QUIZ:

What do Prince Charles and the Roman Emperor Diocletian have in common?

ANSWER: They both love(d) gardening. Diocletian found raising vegetables more satisfying than being emperor. Prince Charles said he likes feeling the earth between his fingers.

Focus on enjoying what you do, not on getting ahead. If you relish your work and give your best effort, you might get ahead. Or you might not. Either way, you'll be happy, and isn't that what counts?

How do you spell $ucce$$?

Bhutan has the philosophy of development aimed at promoting Gross National Happiness, not just Gross National Product.

—Bhutan Ministers' Council Chairman Yeshey Zimba

The most obvious benefit of climbing the career ladder is the booty. To hear politicians and business leaders speak, you would think we starve for money. Remember when President George Bush the First said, "We're enjoying sluggish times and not enjoying them very much." But one thing we can say about North America is that we are splashing about in a sea of money and the material excesses it buys. Sadly, as gross national product more than doubled in the past 50 years, gross national happiness actually decreased.

Studies show that meaning in life and happiness are essential to the concept of the good life. Money makes little difference—despite the efforts of politicians stuck on the standard of living treadmill.

Master salesman Craig Proctor understands this. He sells houses—more than 400 each year. With a gold mine like that, he can also sell his system. Hundreds of real estate agents from across North America attend his seminars. Many of them buy his coaching service. His students become leaders in their field. But it's not the money or the things money can buy that hook them. It's the extra free time with the kids, month-long vacations, relaxing weekends, reclaiming life. That's what's in it for them.

How many people pray almost daily to strike the Big Yahoo in the lottery? It doesn't occur to them that winning would not make them happy, does it? Darlene Daley won the Ohio Lottery jackpot. The $2 million came in handy, thank you very much, but it turns out she is still the same person she was before. A study by the Ontario Lottery Corporation reveals that 85 percent of winners make no major change in lifestyle.

Big bucks won't move your stones. Amazing. Think about all the money spent selling us a vision of how our lives could improve if only, if only... And think about how much we spend on lottery tickets, hoping to "upgrade" our lifestyles. Wow.

The Land of Silk and Money is no Promised Land. Winning huge gobs of cash might actually make a person *less* happy. How can life's simple pleasures hope to measure up to such euphoria? Huge winning. Mega spending. Priceless luxuries. An unhappy poor woman can at least fantasize about striking gold. But if she wins the lottery, what's left when the Big Yahoo fades? An unhappy woman with no more fantasy of happiness, that's what.

Remember King Midas? The Greek God Dionysus granted him the wish of his choice. "I wish that everything I touch turns to gold," he replied with glee (and greed). But when he touched his wife and daughter, their motionless golden figures were of little comfort to him. When all his food also turned to gold, Midas faced starvation. Be careful what you ask for; you might get it.

One Saturday evening, a rich Bel Air couple asked their live-in maid if she would be kind enough to keep her door open. The couple heard the joy and laughter from the maids, the chauffeur, and their friends every Saturday night, and the couple wanted to see it and experience the joy, too. It turns out that the song is wrong: you can't buy the Stairway to Heaven.

So take comfort that Tom Hanks ($71.5 million), Michael Jordan ($30 million before endorsements, just for bouncing and throwing a ball), and Claudia Schiffer ($9 million just for walking and wearing makeup) are no happier than you for all their money.

∞ *The root of all evil* ∞

I bought a ticket for $100, thinking I would be giving $100 to charity—now I can give $1 million.

—Heart and Stroke Foundation lottery winner Gerald Swan

POP QUIZ:
Is money the root of all evil?
ANSWER: Not according to the Bible. It says, "The love of money" is the root of all evil (1 Timothy, 6:10).

Financial guru Michael Phillips calls money a nightmare: "Eighty percent of people in jail are there because of money-related crimes...robbery, burglary, larceny, forgery, and auto theft."

Many Americans fear greed has overtaken respect, honesty, and community participation. Greed, researchers suggest, is not the desire for money; greed is placing more importance on money than on values. Americans' fears might be justified. In 1975, just 38 percent of Americans said they want to earn "a lot of money." By 1994, 63 percent said so.

We measure our wealth against ever-swelling expectations...and can we ever inflate expectations! People living in ghettos and low-income housing projects today own more TVs, VCRs, and designer clothes than did suburbanites of 50 years ago.

We don't feel satisfied—no matter how much we accumulate. Billions of dollars of advertising conspire to convince us we need the latest toothpaste, car, snack, cosmetic, or gadget to be happy. And we feel inadequate for not having it. Now isn't that the ultimate irony? The advertising that tells us how to be happy is, in fact, a major cause of unhappiness.

The hell-bent pursuit of money and possessions has been dubbed "affluenza." Ever wonder how some families seem so content on less than $20,000 per year? Broke, but content.

Other families can't seem to pay the bills on more than $200,000. They complain about the cost of milk and gasoline. They complain about high taxes. And they actually sound poor, despite their affluence. No wonder—imagine the burden of belonging to all the right social clubs, sending the kids to all the right schools, and wearing all the right labels. Aw shucks, doesn't that just bring a tear to your eye? No? Well it should. They might have all the money you wish you had, but, if their expectations rise with their income, they don't appreciate it. The moral of the story is this: don't let your income determine your outcome. And here's a bonus: unlike income, happiness is tax-free.

Money can't buy happiness. Well, actually it can. On Skid Row, a little extra money can make a big difference. Wealth and health share this in common: they don't bring joy, but their absence can leave pure misery.

And sometimes money releases the happiness genie from the bottle. Claude Monet won 100,000 francs in the 1891 French lottery. It allowed him to quit his job and paint, which is what he yearned to do. So money can be useful. The love of money, however, is the root of all evil.

What's in your toy box?

I don't know whether it's the finest public housing in America or the crown jewel of prison life. It's a very isolating life.

—President Bill Clinton, describing life in the White House

"Whoever dies with the most toys wins." You've probably read the bumper sticker. You probably even laughed. Okay, more likely you groaned. But many of us live our lives that way.

Life is not a stockpiling contest. There are a handful of things we really need. Food, clothing, shelter, water. The rest is extra. Everything else is a bonus. Aren't we lucky!

Unfortunately, we have come to expect more. We feel entitled. Instead of appreciating the bounty we have, we covet things we don't have.

Phi Theta Kappa Advisor Don Foran calls "obscene" ads proclaiming that "a Rolex watch is the ultimate expression of love," or, "Prove your love to her; buy her diamonds." Your goal should not be to collect all the multiple-choice stones; it should be to move them from the Wall to your Stairway. Stones in your pocket are worth, well, stones in your pocket. But on your Stairway, you can stand on them and reach Heaven.

One young girl from London, Ontario, puts things in perspective: "Maybe you adults buy Beanie Babies in order to make money, but we kids buy them because we like them. I'm glad I'm a kid."

Exercise:

Write down a list of the things you feel you need beyond food, shelter, and clothing. A lawn tractor? An espresso machine? Embroidered pillow slips? Candles? This list will be useful later on in the book, so write it down now.

The happiest people are not those who *have* the best of everything, but those who *make* the best of everything. They move the stones from the Great Wall of Misery to their Stairways to Heaven. If you focus on stockpiling money or possessions, you'll have a hard time making the nine habits work for you.

∞ *Lookit me, lookit me* ∞

If they even awarded me an Oscar Meyer wiener
for being part of this film, I'd be happy!

—actor Will Smith on his role in the movie *The Legend of Bagger Vance*

Kids say what they mean. "Look at me! Look what I did." They demand praise. Adults are more demure. We want admiration, but we don't ask for it outright. Why? Fame is a fantasy many people harbor. Fame brings happiness, doesn't it? Well, no. The evidence is that happy, famous people are happy despite their fame, not because of it.

Fame fosters pressure to excel, to win, to be perfect. That pressure often hits a star when she's just a child. Examples abound: film stars like Judy Garland, sports idols like figure skater Oksana Baiul, singers like Billie Holiday.

Fame also robs you of your privacy. Monica Lewinsky tries to "pretend that I don't notice that anybody notices me." Meryl Streep seeks out neighborhoods where stars don't normally tread, just to avoid recognition. Oprah Winfrey says, "I've developed a great respect for fish, I'll tell ya, because I've lived my life in a fish bowl."

The need for recognition can also distract us from our path to happiness. Like money, recognition has its place. But like the love of money, the *need* for recognition breeds misery.

⊗ *Are you making a living...or making a dying?* ⊗

At least part of the reason why most seniors turn out to have a strong sense of subjective well-being is that many of the doleful or querulous members of their birth cohort have died off!

—happiness researcher David Lykken

Death is the ultimate culmination of life. Contrary to what the Egyptian pharaohs believed, you really can't take it with you. Whatever lies beyond, you can't take fame. You can't take wealth. You can't take the toys. At the end of the chess game, the kings and the pawns are tossed into the same wooden box.

You might have heard of the multimillionaire who died in his sleep. The tabloids pestered his son, "How much did he leave?" His son responded, "He left it all." Or as Alexander the Great's epitaph reads: "A tomb now suffices for whom the whole world was not sufficient."

Who can forget the poignant scene of Citizen Kane on his deathbed recalling not the newspaper empire he built as an adult, but a toy he played with as a child?

Many religions say we can take our spirit, but none say we can take status with us. Status. That's what all the standard measures of success amount to. Excelling in one's career usually means taking more money, which means buying a bigger house, a fancier car, the latest fashions. We toil for these Masks of Success. By flaunting our status, we impress other people.

It makes sense. If your neighbor is an architect, how do you know if she's a good architect? If he's an accountant, how can you tell if he's a good accountant? If he's an engineer, how would you guess if he's a good engineer?

The only way an outsider can recognize a person's career value is by income, and the only way to evaluate income is by the house, the car, the fashions. After selling his company for nearly $6 billion, former Internet tycoon Mark Cuban explains, "Money is a scoreboard where you can rank how you're doing against other people." While you're still alive, that is.

∾ *How do YOU define success?* ∾

*I'd rather be a failure at something I enjoy
than a success at something I hate.*

—comedian George Burns.

So how do *you* define success? There are countless answers to this question, but they all boil down to just two. You can define success as impressing yourself: that you are happy, that you stand by your values, that you feel fulfilled, that you love. Or you can define success as impressing others: that you have fame, status, money, toys, or even the appearance of a happy family. These are the Masks of Success peddled by the Merchants of Misery.

Peggy Moylan, a senior vice president of advertising giant J. Walter Thompson, was asked about success: "That is a judgement other people make about you. This is my life, I focus more on being happy."

But how do you recognize success when you see it? When have you "made it"? How much is enough? When Julia Roberts accepted the part of Erin Brockovich, she decided it would be the last role she would play for a while, the culminating experience she had worked toward.

Internet entrepreneur Greg Gianforte knew how much is enough. With a wife and kids, life on the road five days a week was just too grueling. "At some point we drew the finish line—the point at which we knew we'd had enough."

Most of us can't stop, even if we accumulate more than we had ever dreamed of. Once on the speeding treadmill, the only answer to "How much is enough?" seems to be, "More."

Charlie was fishing at the end of a pier in a quiet Tennessee lake. Every time he caught a fish, he would throw it back in the water. A stranger had been watching. "Why do you keep throwing away the fish?" he asked.

"I don't need them," Charlie answered.

"But you could sell them," the stranger replied.

"Why would I want to do that?" Charlie asked.

"Well, then you could buy yourself better rods and more bait," the stranger replied.

"Why?" Charlie persisted.

"To catch more fish."

"Why?"

"To make more money, of course."

"Why?"

"So you can expand your business and make even more money," the stranger declared.

"Why would I want to do that?" Charlie wanted to know.

"So you can afford to spend all the time you like out here fishing," replied the exasperated stranger.

"But I already do that," Charlie replied. And he paid no more attention to the frustrated stranger.

All through this chapter, we've seen examples of how happiness grows from within. If we keep pursuing "success," thinking it will make us happy, we risk being all the more unhappy. Doing things to become more successful is a fabulous way to avoid doing things that could really create happiness.

In the end, most people secure from life what they want. They might think they want something else—happiness, for instance—but if they pursue goals that lead in another direction…

You have only one life to live. This is not a dress rehearsal. You get no second chance. The choice is yours.

POP QUIZ:
Remember how we talked about death earlier on. We even read Alexander the Great's epitaph. Here are two tombstone inscriptions. Which one do you want written on yours?
1. A person who spread joy far and near.
2. Rich and impressed people far and near.
Hint: There is no right answer. This one's up to you.

Sarah Sheep is not yet ready to die, and I presume you are not either. She knows the meaning of success. She knows how much is enough. When she escapes the well she fell into, that will be enough. Set your sights on what you really mean by "success."

The habits in this book will work for you only if you let happiness grow inside you. You have to decide which is more important to you—happiness or success. Money is handy. Toys can be useful. Recognition is rewarding. But they cannot carry you around the Wall. If they distract you from building your Stairway, the Merchants of Misery will defeat your quest for happiness.

Already you have advanced further in this book than you might think. You are now able to recognize the difference between what you can and cannot change—which stones you can move from the Great Wall of Misery to your Stairway to Heaven. You can unmask the Merchants of Misery who try to distract you from building your Stairway. Your tools are the nine habits of maximum happiness. In the next chapter, let's find out why these tools are so useful. Then you'll be ready to start building your Stairway with them.

Exercise:

Write down the five most important things in your life— the things that at the end of your life you want to have achieved. They might be career, family, church, character, hobbies, charity, whatever. Then list the steps you have to take to be successful for each item. This is your life plan for success. This is how you define success.

RES:

FAMILY → COMMUNICATION + MEET. SHARE LOVE + GRATITUDE
FRIENDS → BUILD OWN FAMILY
NURTURE GOOD RELATIONSHIPS THROUGH DOING
JOB SATISFACTION → ENJOY THE RIGHT THINGS / VALUES.
HOBBIES → HAVE BY WHAT I DO.
MYSELF TO ENJOY VARIETY OF PASTTIMES +
SOCIAL CONTRIBUTION ENRICH MYSELF
→ GIVE BACK TO SOCIETY / OTHER LESS FORTUNATE / TRY TO DRIVE
POSITIVE CHANGES IN PEOPLES ATTITUDES / BEHAVIOURS.

CHAPTER 3

Making happiness a habit

Between saying and doing, many a pair of shoes is worn out.

—Italian proverb

Bray Goat faces a challenge. After all, he's just a silly old goat. Shaking off stones and stepping up does not come naturally to him. He has to stop and think about it each time. That presents a challenge.

Life is a do-it-yourself project, and this is your blueprint for happiness. You supply the hammer and chisel and shovel and brute force to lift the stones from the Wall to your Stairway. This book is your guide to moving the stones. But let's face it, the book will not move the stones. That's your job as stonemason, and the nine habits are your power tools.

Bray Goat and Sarah Sheep eventually discover that shaking off stones and stepping onto them becomes a habit if they keep at it. With time, they no longer have to think about what to do. That leaves them with more energy to shake their backs and lift their legs. As you develop habits, it will become easier for you, too. The power of habits!

Happiness is not a product of habits alone, of course. Both the Great Wall of Misery and your Stairway to Heaven are built from various kinds of stones. For instance, character traits play a role in your happiness. Researchers identify four character traits common to most happy people: a sense of control, an optimistic outlook, high self-esteem, and an extroverted personality.

Most of the habits in this book actually help you build on those character traits if you have them, or create them if you don't. (That's a bonus offer you didn't even have to pay for. Now doesn't that make you feel happy?)

Happiness also flows from life strategies. You can make decisions about these, too. Do you wish to be an office clerk or a movie stunt person? Do you choose a hermit's life on a secluded island, or do you prefer to raise nine children in a bustling household? Is your notion of bliss a couch, a blanket, and the remote control, or do you prefer skiing and scuba diving?

We won't talk about life strategies in this book. Those are habitat stones, and they are far too personal for a book to guide you. Habits, on the other hand, can help you be happier, whatever life strategy you choose.

Knowledge also favors happiness. The brain burns 15 calories each hour, whether thinking or idling, so you might as well use it.

But knowledge alone will not make you happy. Consider Loretta LaRoche, a Boston area lecturer on stress and humor. She recounts how she and her husband, a stress management consultant, start a vacation by getting all hot under the collar over change at a tollbooth. Their knowledge about stress management did help them get past the incident and laugh about it, but that knowledge did not exempt them from basic emotions.

In another instance, Harvard social psychologist Roger Brown recalls driving into a narrow street just as another car turned into the opposite end. They "came at one another like two combative mice, getting angrier as we approached, until at close quarters I recognized a colleague." At that moment, anger switched to smiles. Despite his education and profession as a psychologist, he was not exempt from the power of emotions.

No matter how much you learn from this book, you will benefit primarily when you form habits from the information. That's why we focus on habits—not traits, not life strategies, not knowledge. Habits help you move the stones to your Stairway to Heaven so you can climb up on top.

Some books on happiness pretend they can cover everything that affects our happiness. This book covers only those areas you can improve through habits. Here are a few of the issues I chose not to cram into these pages: (Although I do make references to some of them in the context of issues I do cover.)

• Psychological disorders
• Religion and spirituality
• Height
• Birth order
• Geography
• Age
• Romance and marriage
• Gender
• Addictions

Why do I leave these out? The obvious reason is with everything about happiness, you'd need a Hercules and three forklifts to pick up the book. After all, this is not a muscle-building exercise; it's a blueprint for your Stairway to Heaven. Books that try to cover too much cover each subject too little.

Let's focus here on the nine habits—habits you can use every day of your life. Applying these habits can make you happier than winning the lottery, and I'll tell you why in the next few pages.

⟨⟩ *Flights and trenches* ⟨⟩

*My definition of the good life is not the massive
and unrepeatable extravagance,
but a gradual accumulation of habits, friends and possessions…
that provide regular and sustained joy.*

—writer Peter Mayle

POP QUIZ:
The higher you fly, the harder you fall. True or false?
ANSWER: True. Researchers say you cannot predict that a person will suffer little bad feeling just because he enjoys plenty of good feelings. In other words, thrills and fun do not chase away the blues. If you tend to feel more intense positive emotions, you'll also feel more intense negative emotions.

Some people look for happiness in fun. If they could just enjoy enough thrilling experiences, they are convinced they would be happier. They are wrong. Very wrong. In fact, the more thrilling experiences you collect, the harder you might have to toil to overcome those experiences…if you want to be happy.

Now, I know you might be saying, "The fool author's talking nonsense." Let me assure you: you won't build your Stairway to Heaven jumping from airplanes or riding roller coasters. You might have fun. You'll definitely get a thrill. But following the volatile life-is-a-carnival philosophy is not the path to happiness.

Young people often fly to heights of joy and dig trenches to the depths of despair, but such extremes are not sustainable—not if one plans to be happy. As Professor Sandra Marie Schneider told students at their commencement, "This is a very significant moment in your life, too significant, I think, to be rushed through in such a blur of excitement that the deeper meaning of it all is missed."

In Chapter 2, remember how lottery winners were no happier once the initial euphoria wore off? Intense joy impedes a person's ability to appreciate so many mildly positive things in his life. For instance, it feels great to fall head over heels in love (especially if you're a contortionist), but falling in love is like winning the jackpot. What happens when the initial euphoria wears off? Are you still *in* love? Or do you just love? Or is there nothing left but a pulse? If you aim for the thrill, you'll be left empty-hearted. If you aim for the long-term love, you might just walk away a winner.

Fun and thrills are just hit-and-run happiness. If a person was unhappy to begin with, she'll be unhappy again when the thrill is over. Happiness and unhappiness are pervasive. They are chronic. They last through hard knocks and tough shocks, through great fun and the bright sun.

I remember the thrill of seeing snow in the Mojave Desert. I'm from up north, so snow is no big deal for me. But the last place I expected snow was tucked up against the cactus and the Joshua tree of southern California. But alas, the snow did not last. It melted quickly.

POP QUIZ:
What's the difference between a mural and a fresco? Both are wall paintings, right?

ANSWER: Murals are like fun; you can remove them by peeling or scraping. They vanish on the heels of a Mojave snowfall. Frescos form an integral part of the wall; like happiness, they endure. They are more like the glaciers of Alaska.

One lady described her mountain-climbing experience in Maine as "exhilarating." When she reached the summit, though, she broke out in tears, and her tears "definitely weren't tears of joy."

My wife, Chantal, is one of those people whose emotions swing wildly. She savors great joy (which makes her quite attractive), but she also "crashes." That's where I come in. My job is to be her trampoline—to help her bounce back out of the trench as quickly as possible. That's one reason why Chantal and I enjoy life more now than before we met...but that's another book.

⚭ *Chronic happiness* ⚭

Enthusiasm is the electricity of life. How do you get it?
You act enthusiastic until you make it a habit.

—photographer Gordon Parks

There is no elevator to Heaven. You have to build your Stairway one stone at a time. Your best bet is to aim for chronic happiness, a lasting sense of contentment, rather than acute happiness based primarily on one-time events. One study reveals how daily pleasant events even boosts our immune systems.

To be chronically happier, raise your day-to-day happiness level. That's where habits come in. (Yes, we're almost there now.) Habits are what we do every day, the things we do even when our brains take a leave of absence. We give a lot of thought to them at first, of course, but after a while they become habits. (That's why we call them habits, in case you were wondering.) Some habits gel after just a few dozen repetitions. Others take longer, especially if they must replace old, deeply ingrained habits. When we get there, we live in our *habit*at.

We've talked a lot about building habits for happiness. One goal of each new habit we apply is to replace a bad habit—one that separates us from happiness. Do you recognize this process? We move stones one at a time from the Great Wall of Misery to your Stairway to Heaven. Each time you apply a habit, think of it—visualize it—as a stone you remove from the Wall and place on your Stairway.

This takes work. Habits don't just pop up like the flowers that bloom in the spring. Be like a river. Through habit, the river cuts through the rocks in the long run. That's how the Grand Canyon was formed, persistently carving through the hardest stone one drop at a time. Habits can build your Stairway to Heaven.

Once upon a time, a wise king plunked a boulder on the path to his castle to see who would remove it. Lords and ladies stepped around it. They indignantly blamed the king for not clearing the road, but nobody lifted a finger to move the stone. They were burdened by the useless habit of complaining about things they didn't like.

A peasant girl carrying two buckets of water plodded by. Setting the buckets aside, the girl struggled to move the boulder. She was blessed with the useful habit of fixing things she didn't like. With some difficulty, she moved the stone. As she picked up her buckets, something caught her eye. A small purse lay where the boulder had stood. Peering inside the purse, the peasant girl found 20 gold coins and a note from the king: "To ye who move the boulder, be filled with joy."

For all their money and status, the miserable lords and ladies were too busy complaining. They stepped around the boulder, but they did not step around the Wall. The peasant girl focused on doing what she believed she should, and, by moving the stone, she climbed higher on her Stairway. Same boulder, different actions. Same problem, different reactions. Good habits: that's the difference between misery and happiness.

My friend, Peter, likes to recall the biblical tale of Nehemiah, who sets out to fix the broken wall of the city. Stone by stone, he rebuilds the wall. Enemies try to discourage him, but he ignores them. They try to frustrate his efforts, but he ignores them. He just keeps moving his stones and rebuilding the Wall.

The U.S. Constitution guarantees the pursuit of happiness. It's up to you to pursue it. Now let me offer you fair warning. Getting started is easy. Replacing old habits with new ones is a cinch…until a moment of stress or a distraction. Quitting smoking, dieting, starting an exercise routine seem easy at first, but they are deceptively challenging.

Sarah Sheep found it easy to shake off the first few stones. But as more stones slam down on her back and her head, her task grows harder and harder.

Replacing unhappy habits with happy habits requires both the initial commitment and ongoing effort until the new habits are 100 percent ingrained. We live in a world of instant gratification, fast-food results, just-in-time delivery, real-time profits…where change strikes with the pop of a pill. Happiness is not like that. Your happy habitat must be built one stone at a time.

Are you ready to start moving the stones? You know what you can and cannot change, you recognize the Merchants of Misery, and you understand how habits make the difference. You are now ready to use the tools—the nine habits of maximum happiness.

Let's get to it.

PART II

HAPPY WITH YOURSELF

HABIT # 1

Throw a parade in your honor

If we cannot do what we will, we must do what we can.

—Yiddish proverb

You are a winner. Maybe you feel like one and maybe you don't. But you are. The first habit to be happier is to feel like a winner. You are more than just a stonemason in this book; you are the victor, the hero. Ta-dah! If you see yourself as a victor, this part will be easy. If you do not, this part is absolutely necessary.

Bray Goat is losing steam. He keeps shaking off stones and stepping up. Shaking off stones and stepping up. Shaking off stones and stepping up. Yet he feels like a failure. So many stones, such tired bones. And the mouth of the well—Heaven—seems so far away. Bray Goat feels like a loser, a victim.

Losers don't feel happy. Remember how to scale the Great Wall of Misery to reach the Green Pastures of Cloud Nine? Move the multiple-choice stones from the Wall to your Stairway to Heaven. Several stones are marked with a ♥. You decide if the ♥ stands for "victim" or for "victor" by where you place the stone.

Try this. Think about your day. Let me give you just a few examples from mine:

- A car nearly hit me.
- I tried to send a fax, but I couldn't feed the page.
- I treated myself to a muffin and orange juice.
- I chatted with a friend about current events.
- I met someone who might help me with a future project.
- I ate a healthy lunch.
- I put my sock on backwards. I wasted time putting it back on right.
- I brushed my teeth.
- I wrote a long-overdue letter.

The complete list would fill this book. Some things I did today were useful and pleasant. Others were frustrating and unpleasant. Every day, we do things we like and things we dislike. They are not good things. They are not bad things. They are things we choose to like or dislike.

POP QUIZ:

When the car almost hits me, how should I react? Should I wave my fist and shout, "Watch where you're going, Bozo-breath!" After all, the stupid driver nearly killed me. Or should I grin and think, "Saved by an angel. Thank God I braked in time." After all, I have every right to smile; I saved my life.

ANSWER: Rage or smile—either way, it's your right. It's your right to be miserable. It's your right to be happy. It really is your choice. But if you choose to feel like a victim, don't expect to be happy, too.

Do you truly celebrate all your victories, even the small ones? Habit #1 is to throw a parade in honor of you, the victor, so you can march triumphantly up your Stairway to Heaven.

CHAPTER 4

Scraping the bug off the windshield

*The best place to find a helping hand
is at the end of your own arm.*

—Swedish proverb

How do you see yourself? Are you the windshield or the bug? The windshield ploughs through just about anything. The bug goes **SPLAT!!!** Maybe it seems like you splat more often than not. Who would be happy splatting all over the place?

People with low self-esteem often feel like the bug. They associate failure with rejection. We all know what it's like to be accepted conditionally, but when this state of mind prevails…**SPLAT!**

Exercise:
How many diseases and colds and flues did you catch? Think about how many you pulled through. Write them down for future reference. How many falls and slips and crashes did you endure? You survived them all. How many injuries and bruises and aches and pains did you suffer? Now think about how few of them killed you. Wow. You're no bug. You don't go splat. You're the victor. You would need a lifetime to recall all your death-defying victories.

So why does the victor feel like a bug so often? Maybe the role of victim attracts sympathy— "aawww... the poor martyr." Or maybe it's the lazy person's way to avoid responsibility. The role of victim is comfortable and safe...and we all have a lazy side to us.

Whatever the reason, we don't want any victims in this book. Devictimification is the goal of this chapter. If you can pronounce that word from the Dictionary of David, give yourself two bonus points. There you go, another victory to celebrate.

⁓ *Victims of venomous fate* ⁓

The object of war is to survive it.

—author John Irving

Are you a victim of venomous fate? Do you suffer from everybody's ingratitude, treachery, rudeness, disrespect? It's easy to react against things. From the word go, the word was "no." Your parents probably told you "no" a gazillion times when you were young. As an adult we still react against people, events, even things.

Lori worked for weeks choosing menus, arranging decorations, hiring a Santa Claus for the kids, coordinating a gift exchange, gathering music. Every detail was checked and double-checked. The day before the office Christmas party, a competing firm made a surprise bid for her company's biggest client. The staff worked through the night. Nobody was in the mood for a party. Who, including Lori, could have kept their eyes open anyway?

Lori felt deflated. "Why always me?" she asked, recalling one failure after another: the rained-out picnic, young Katie's slanted birthday cake, the back of her skirt tucked up into her pantyhose at the office.

Her husband tried to cheer her up. "What about all the great things you've done?" he asked. "What about the camping trip when we saw the otters? What about the promotion you earned last year?" Lori didn't want to hear about her successes. She was fixated on being a victim. She refused to move her stones, and both she and her husband suffered for it.

Lori is a victim wannabe. Nobody died. Nobody lost a job. It was just a party. There was no real pain, but Lori chose to suffer because events and her expectations chose different paths.

William Smith must have felt like a victim after being elected Lake County Auditor in Illinois. Sure, he won the election, but the voters also abolished the position of Auditor on the same ballot. His reaction? "I feel like I've gone off a diving board and suddenly found the pool was empty." Or like he was flying around and suddenly realized he was a bug. **SPLAT!** Hopefully he later took stock of all his victories, too.

Bad news for victims of venomous fate: it doesn't care about you. Fate is not out to get you. It deals your cards, ups and downs alike, with no regard for your happiness. That's up to you to build.

∞ *You missed a spot* ∞

Excuse the mess, but we live here.

—comedienne Roseanne Barr

It's not always the windshield out to get us. Sometimes we seem to be our own worst enemy. Have you ever felt like Wile E. Coyote, like you just can't do anything right? Like you're trying to ride out a reign of error?

POP QUIZ: ....

Do you qualify for the Darwin Awards?

ANSWER: Not if you're alive. The Darwin Awards honor "the remains of the individuals who contributed to the improvement of our gene pool by removing themselves from it in a really stupid way."

Some Palestinian terrorists transported a pair of bombs a few days before the world switches to Standard Time. Israel switched from Daylight Savings Time early for a week of pre-sunrise prayers. Palestinians turn their noses up at "Zionist Time." The terrorists set their bombs to explode at 5:30 Israeli time, but the drivers had already switched their watches to Standard Time. In two different cities, two different drivers, two different cars… **KA-BOOM!**

I don't know if Frederick won a Darwin Award, but he should have. Suffering from acute bronchitis, he was placed in an oxygen tent. Despite repeated warnings, his desperation for a cigarette got the better of him. Another tale ends in **KA-BOOM!**

Few of us will ever compete for the Darwin Awards. That should make you breathe easier. The next time you goof, think of how insignificant it is. It's not like you're Adam or Eve and you've just condemned humanity to eternal sin.

Yet sometimes we feel like we just can't do anything right. We see other families solve problems in 22 minutes flat. Perfect every time. Welcome to the wonderful world of television sitcoms and other weekly serials. They raise impossible expectations against which we measure our progress. When we appear to fall short, we stomp on our self-esteem by calling it failure.

A case in point: smokers who try to quit, then quit (quit trying to quit) far too soon. It takes on average seven attempts to quit smoking. Don't call the first seven (or more) attempts failures… they are seven steps to success. That's what Thomas Edison called the light bulb and his 100 previous attempts to perfect it: an invention that took 100 steps. He moved his stones by how he reacted to those "failures."

Have you ever heard, "You missed a spot?" You just washed 14 windows, waxed the hardwood floors, painted the ceiling, weeded the garden. But you missed a spot. Hours of work all for naught? Never mind that you can finally see through the windows. Never mind that the floors are now well protected or that only *you* notice the spot of missing paint on the ceiling. Never mind that your healthy garden flourishes. All you feel is spotmisserism. (There's that Dictionary of David again.) But it's all just much ado about almost nothing.

I missed a spot. One Saturday night, flying high above the Atlantic coast, I realized I had forgotten to pack my dress shoes. I was wearing running shoes for the flight, and my speech in Newfoundland was first thing Sunday morning—too early to buy new shoes. Electric panic shot through my veins. Just for a moment, though. Then I thought, "How can I squeeze lemonade out of this lemon?" It was a bit late to reorient my speech to include the running shoes, but that's just what I did. I made them a prop in my speech.

POP QUIZ:
Which makes the biggest **SPLAT!** on your windshield:

A. A mosquito
B. A deer fly
C. A dragon fly
D. A moth

ANSWER: It doesn't matter. It's just a splotch. Wipe it off the windshield. As anthropologist Margaret Mead put it, "You just have to learn not to care about the dust mites under the beds."

One stone sticks on Bray Goat's back. He can't shake it off. And Sarah Sheep is doing all she can just to keep from being buried alive. At first, the stray stone bothers him. But he cannot afford to focus on that stone. He has to keep shaking the others off and stepping up. Otherwise, how could he climb his Stairway to Heaven and escape the well?

Do you expect too much of yourself? Do you expect perfection? Let's face it, none of us are perfect. Why cling to one mistake when we revel in so much we do well? Many of us beat ourselves up for our mistakes. Avoid poop and scoop critiquing. We dump on ourselves, then we pick up the droppings and carry our -CENSORED- around like a trophy. Just flush it. (Now there's a slogan for the 21st century: Just flush it!)

Few of us will ever blunder as badly as Adam and Eve did. The folks at Ford tried in 1948. After deciding that Volkswagen and its Beetle were worthless, and refusing to accept them as part of war reparations, they decided to build instead…the Edsel, one of the biggest flops ever. General Motors tried to out-flop Ford by selling the Chevy Nova in Mexico, not realizing that *no va* means "won't go" in Spanish.

The worst decision ever, in this author's opinion, was to order 20 million tons of cement to build new roads, airfields, and buildings in Nigeria. The country's docks could handle no more than 2,000 tons per day. At one point, the cement sitting in ships just outside of Lagos would have taken 27 years to unload…had much of it not set in the cargo holds first.

Cheer up. You make mistakes. I make mistakes. Don't let life's little gutter balls dampen your mood. To err is human, so err when you must. Leave spotmisserism to someone else. Your Stairway to Heaven will serve you just fine, even with a crack here or a missing stone there.

Pin-the-blame-on-the-donkey

But it really doesn't matter whom you put upon the list,
For they'd none of 'em be missed, they'd none of 'em be missed.

—Gilbert and Sullivan in *The Mikado*

Our culture breeds victims. When not blaming ourselves, we blame somebody else. And there are oodles of people to blame.

Let's see who's playing pin-the-blame-on-the-donkey. Johnny Carson sues Here's Johnny Portable Toilets Inc. Vanna White sues Samsung when a female robot turns over a letter in its ad. Some students in Britain, after failing an exam, sue their teachers for not teaching them well enough. A lady sues the Pennsylvania Lottery Commission because the $150,000 her family spent on lottery tickets yields no winnings.

Tobacco victims are the latest rage. One court ruling awarded $20 million to a lady who smoked from 1972 to 1998. She blamed the cigarette companies for deceiving her about the health effects of smoking. Now, I'm no defender of cigarette makers. When you peddle poison, you get what you deserve. But cigarette packages have featured the Surgeon General's warning since 1969. Even when I was nine years old (just a few years later), I knew smoking was deadly. Can this lady really claim to be a victim?

Now governments, too, are playing pin-the-blame-on-the-tobacco-companies, as if they were innocent bystanders. They had policy options. Are they not, by their inaction, accessories to the very crimes they blame on the cigarette companies?

Which donkey is next? Will someone sue fried chicken restaurants because buckets of fatty food provoke heart attacks? Will someone sue computer makers because staring at a screen for hours on end is unhealthy? Will someone sue McDonald's for serving coffee that's not cold, not tepid, but—heaven forbid—hot? (Oops! That's been done.) The whole world's a target. Blame away!

We could force all knife makers to design blunt knives, and tool companies to make soft hammers, and auto makers to build very, very, very slow cars. Then we might be safe. Of course, we would also want shorter cliffs, slower rivers, and shallower oceans. Hmmmm…I suppose we could still sue somebody for lightening. Look out, God. After all, if a man can sue a coffee shop for trapping his, uh, body part in a toilet seat, who's not a culprit?

Then I read the *New York Times* headline: "Citing Public Nuisance, New York Will Be First State to Sue Gun Makers." Here we go again.

POP QUIZ:
How can you find a donkey to blame?
ANSWER: Just blindfold yourself and strike out in any direction. Pin-the-blame-on-the-donkey is best played with eyes wide shut.

Not long ago, a freak storm stranded me in an airport for eight hours. The pilots—bless their souls—decided not to cast us into the fury of the gale. I was content to wait in the crash-free comfort of the airport.

Not everybody applauded the pilots' wisdom. After a few hours, some would-be passengers grew surly. Their remarks to the airline staff bordered on rude. One nearly lost it: "Aw c'mon. This is ridiculous. Why can't we just get going?" Thankfully, another man said, "Lay off her. Just relax. We're all here together." Then I added, "She's doing the best she can. I, for one, don't want to fly anywhere the pilots don't want to fly." Like the rain itself, these dew stones were soon to evaporate. How easy to find someone to blame, even for a storm blowing through to clean the air and water the plants.

Two medical researchers report that both physical health and emotional well-being suffer when we blame someone else for our misfortunes. It "shatters either the illusion of self-sufficiency or the belief in a benign world and the reliability of others," write Howard Tennen and Glenn Affleck. They also point out how our legal system relies on attributing blame. Another study shows that whiplash injuries heal faster when claims settle faster. The less effort spent on blame, the more remains for healing.

So let's not play pin-the-blame-on-the-donkey when things don't go as expected. We might be right in our cause, but would you rather be right than happy?

∞ *But aren't there real victims?* ∞

I am dying, but otherwise I am quite well.

—British writer Dame Edith Sitwell

You might wonder, "What about real victims?" Stranded for a few hours by a storm might not make me a victim, but what about losing one's home in a storm? What about being injured in a crash? What about the death of one's child? Are there no real victims?

Of course there are. There is *bona fide* pain in life. But pain and suffering are not the same. Pain is inflicted on us. We inflict suffering on ourselves. Sometimes we need to suffer; that's what mourning is about. A real victim mourns, then picks up the pieces and starts rebuilding her life. A victim wannabe just keeps on suffering.

In my line of work as a safety advocate, I sometimes come across genuine tragedy. One woman wrote to me about the loss of her only child in a horrific crash. She would never enjoy grandchildren. "To lose a child is devastating and inconsolable," she wrote. What could I say? I sympathized, I said I could not begin to understand her pain, and I wished her success finding meaning in the loss.

I really felt for the volunteer firefighter in Kansas who arrived at the fiery crash scene to find his son...dead.

Psychology professor Shelley Taylor says that those who are victimized by others suffer most because they can't see meaning in the tragedy. Rape. Incest. Assault. "Why me?" they ask. Sometimes there is no answer.

In most cases, happiness returns to normal by six months after even momentous events. Most people with disabilities, for instance, report normal levels of well-being. A study in Michigan reveals that just three weeks after suffering spinal cord injury, paralyzed victims are generally happy again.

Yes, there are true victims. Some feel like victims. Some don't. And then there are the rest of us. Some of us feel like victims. Some of us don't. Some stones in the Wall just will not budge. But those multiple-choice stones—your reactions to the ricochets of life—can move. The choice is yours.

Sarah Sheep and Bray Goat made the choice. They have no time to feel like victims. They either victoriously climb their Stairway to Heaven or suffocate as victims under a pile of stones. Being a victim does not interest them one bit.

A "victim" is not in control of her life. And a sense of control is vital for happiness. You can make a choice only when you feel in control. If you feel like a victim…**SPLAT!**

Let go of the victim label. Except in the most extreme cases, when you need to mourn, you should feel like the victor—not the victim, not the bug. And when you need to mourn, do so with all your heart. When your heart is cleansed, put it behind you and focus on your happiness—and the happiness of everyone around you.

Exercise:

Do you feel victimized by anyone or anything? Make a list of what you feel victimizes you. Ask yourself what it would take to bring closure to each item and walk away a victor. Save this list for later.

CHAPTER 5

Your cheering squad (Yay!)

Trust in Allah, but tie your camel first.

—Arabic proverb

Hip hip hooray! If feeling like a victim blocks your view of happiness, feeling like a victor lifts you up onto your Stairway to Heaven. You don't need to copy Joan of Arc or Alexander the Great. You don't have to beat anybody. Everything we do in life, from waking up in the morning to raising our children, from solving a riddle to earning a promotion—everything we do is a challenge. And every challenge we confront is our victory cheer. Yay!

POP QUIZ:
Who should lead your cheering squad?
ANSWER: You, of course. If you don't cheer for you, who will? You have to be your own yayist. Take a bow as you soak up the critical acclaim.

Ashley is a real estate agent. Over the years, she sold thousands of homes across New Jersey. She kept a binder with photographs of every house she sold, but somehow she just never felt she amounted to much. "I sell houses. So what?"

One day, Ashley's daughter Jenny came home from school with an assignment to report on a parent's career. Jenny asked for photos that Ashley had not yet placed in the binder. From these Jenny selected the 10 most recent sales, kissed her mother, and ran off.

Three weeks later, Jenny burst into the house. "Mom, I got an A on my project," she hollered, sliding it onto the kitchen table and bounding upstairs to change. Ashley went over to the table and opened the cover to read the title of Jenny's project: *My Mom Gives Homes to People.* As Ashley opened the cover, she saw on each page a picture of a house she had sold... and two or three pictures of the families who now call those houses home.

**WANTED -
CHEERLEADERS**
Now hiring! Cheerleaders for self-cheering. Must be able to identify success in all situations. Capable of forgiving errors. On call 24 hours.

For the first time, Ashley recognized her value. From that day forward, Ashley keeps a photograph of each house she sells *and* a photograph of each family that makes it home.

Exercise:

Think about all of your accomplishments. Make a list. Do you have a family? Do you love them? Do you take care of them? Do you serve your clientele well at work? Do you help build your community? Do you help your neighbors? There's plenty to be proud of. Revel in your accomplishments. Three cheers for you. Hip hip hooray! Add those stones to your Stairway.

∽ *Positive illusions* ∽

They've got us surrounded again, the poor bastards.

—U.S. General Creighton W. Abrams

Confident in their knowledge, experts reject phrases like, "I was almost wrong." They simply know they are right. When they err, they tend to say, "I was almost right." This is how they cheer for themselves. Psychologists call such statements "positive illusions." I simply call them yayisms.

Would you believe that Olympic bronze medallists feel happier than silver medallists? The silver medallists can taste the gold they fail to achieve, but the bronze medallists just thank the stars above for the medal they manage to secure.

You might be tempted to view positive illusions as merely minor disagreements with reality. When the gravity of the situation weighs you down, why not use positive illusions? Why not climb your Stairway? Why not just defy gravity? Maybe you are among those who already use the self-serving bias of positive illusions, taking credit for what works and ascribing to fate what does not. "I was really up on my game" works for victory, but "The sun was in my eyes" works better in defeat. At least out loud. Inside, we might still blame ourselves.

Blame does not help, whether we feel like a loser at our own hands or a victim of venomous fate. When change is needed, by all means, take responsibility and make the change. But when change is not required, why blame? Blame bogs you down and makes a loser out of a winner. Why feel like a loser? So you were off on your game. That happens. Enough said (and enough thought, too).

Tycoon Malcolm Forbes said, "If you expect nothing, you're apt to be surprised. You'll get it." What happens in your head affects what happens to your body. The pessimist might be right in the long run, but it's the yayist who enjoys the trip. And why not? The yayist's trip is a parade up his Stairway to Heaven. So if you want to "live long and prosper," start cheering your parade.

POP QUIZ: ....
Success has a million fathers, but failure is an orphan. True or false?
ANSWER: True…at least in public. But sometimes we internally nurture our failures more than our successes. We have to proclaim our victories internally as much as we do to others—more so, in fact.

Failure need not be an orphan, nor should failure mean feeling like a loser. We learn our most important lessons when we're so deep in you-know-what that we need hip-waders. Cheer for your failures. That's how to move your stones.

Cher, a popular singer who slipped into obscurity and arose again as a superstar, says, "Rejection and failure are a really valuable part of life. You might have to go back five steps, but if you can go ahead six, that's one step you're ahead." Cher cheered her failures and moved her stones.

As Muhammad Ali noted, "Ain't nothing wrong with going down. It's staying down that's wrong." Cheer your failures as your successes. That's a positive illusion that will serve you well.

∞ *Don't take it personally* ∞

I phoned my dad to tell him I had stopped smoking.
He called me a quitter.

—actor Steven Pearl

One way to propel your parade is to not let negatives bug you—don't take them personally. The world is not a windshield out to splat you. And not everything is your fault. The newsletter *Customer Service* offers this stress management tip: "If someone has a problem with a product or service, don't make it your personal problem. If a customer gets angry at you or becomes verbally abusive, remember that this person's emotions are directed at the product or service you are associated with, not at you."

"They" are not out to get you. You don't even figure into their thought process. When someone cuts in front of you at the checkout line or on the highway, she is not trying to upset you. When someone complains about your loud voice, cigarette smoke, or ugly tattoo, he is not trying to ruin your life.

Psychology professor Jeffrey Kottler recounts his days as a rookie therapist. He felt "awkward and confused" struggling to help his clients solve simple troubles, while recalling the puzzling plights his mentors seemed to solve with ease. As a student, the cases he read about in textbooks were all confusing, but the authors always knew exactly what to do. They never wrote about their losses or failures. Choose the right comparisons and feel like a victor. Choose the wrong ones and feel like the bug. Don't take it personally. Don't let it bug you.

The corollary to not taking things too personally is to not take yourself too seriously. Garth Boyce and Jimmie Taylor were both running for town council in Texas. Either they both ran equally superb campaigns, or they made equally poor pitches; the vote was a tie. So they agreed to flip a coin. One won. One lost. Life goes on.

∞ *You feelin' lucky?* ∞

Today so far, I had a good day. I got a dial tone.

—comedian Rodney Dangerfield

People who believe they are lucky feel less anxiety and less depression. We don't need a horseshoe or a rabbit's foot to feel lucky. Just appreciate the good things you do, the positive things that happen to you, how much turns out right. Practice yayism.

Your parents raised you and they made mistakes. How do I know? Was I there? Of course not. But everybody errs. That's one of the lessons in Chapter 4. Your parents made mistakes, but you turned out fine, right? (I can safely make that assumption because my market research reveals that very few serial murderers are likely to read my book.)

You didn't order 20 million tons of cement, did you? Or build the Edsel, or blow yourself up because you can't tell time? See, you don't do too badly. Your mistakes are minor. Did you wonder why I shared with you those examples of world-class boo-boos? Now you have a basis for comparison. Next time you think, "Oh oh, I've gone and done it again," relax. You live a charmed life. Your errors will never compare to the screw-ups in Chapter 4. Aren't you the lucky one!

> **How and "Y" to cheer?**
>
> Yay for good deeds you do.
> Yee-haw for somebody close.
> Yippee for the meal you make.
> Yes! for a new day.
> Yahoo for a job well done.

⚭ *Aren't there real victors?* ⚭

*Sometimes a negative can be a positive
and a positive can be an opportunity.*

—Kathrine Switzer, first woman to run an official marathon

In the previous chapter, we asked, "Aren't there real victims?" Yes, there are. Now we ask, "Aren't there real victors?" Yes, there are, and you can be one of them.

Start building your Stairway by how you react to daily events. You decide to count each one among either your victories or your defeats. Think about how frustrated you get when a computer (fax machine/store clerk/bank machine/voice mail/pick your demon) does not respond the way you expect. That little, tiny, insignificant weed in the garden of life can upset you, maybe even ruin your day. Are you like most people? Do you make a big deal of a few little defeats?

Now think about your victories. You tell a funny joke. You help a colleague. You learn more about the world in a newspaper. You fix your son's toy. Your lungs draw a deep breath of fresh air. These are the victories of everyday life. These are the ingredients for chronic happiness—a lasting happy habitat. Do you celebrate them? Do you roll out the red carpet? Do you throw a parade in honor of your great deeds and proclaim this *(place your name here)* Day? No? Why not? If we don't celebrate our frequent victories, but wallow in the odd defeat, how can we be happy?

Sometimes we think we fail without a really big success. Have you ever seen Frank Capra's *It's a Wonderful Life*? George Bailey focuses on that one big goal he never achieves: to escape his one-horse town. He fails to see that his life is one glorious triumph after another. It's an easy mistake to make.

Scores of your multiple-choice stones are marked with a **V**. But is it a **V** for "victim" or a **V** for "victory"? When the stones are victims, they rest on the Great Wall of Misery. When they are victories, they form part of your Stairway to Heaven, and you can triumphantly step up on top of them. As long as we feel like victims, we can't be happy, we can't be satisfied, we can't feel the joy of life. Why? Because too much joy would challenge our illusion of victimhood.

From victim to victor

We are so outnumbered there's only one thing to do.
We must attack.

—British World War II admiral Sir Andrew Cunningham

As with other aspects of your happiness, ask the question: "Who runs my life?" The answer should be you. You are in control. You can choose to feel lucky, or optimistic, or happy. You can choose the role of victor.

This is why the role of victim is dangerous. A victim is someone who cedes control to others, a mere pawn on the chessboard of life. A victim cannot choose to be happy. You do not want to be a victim. Some things don't turn out the way you plan. Does that make you a victim? Or do you take the next step to accept/reverse/reorient/ignore what went wrong?

Following the senseless death of a road construction worker at the hands of a sleeping driver, the coroner convened an inquest. I was among those called to testify. The family of the victim participated with "standing"—as a formal party to the inquest. I was amazed at how the wife and daughter carried themselves. They formed a construction zone safety group. They conducted research. They did whatever they could to ensure their beloved did not die in vain. They found a way to give his death meaning. Sure, they still missed him. But they did not allow their loss to make them victims. They recast themselves as survivors, even victors. They moved their stones.

Meaning is harder for victims of domestic violence to find. This is equally true for male victims as for female victims, by the way, who feel shame admitting their wives overpower them. Peter Olszewski was such a victim. When he finally spoke about his experience on an Australian radio program, he fielded calls for weeks from battered men who felt they had nobody to talk to. "While time consuming, this was very beneficial for me because I went from being a victim to being a survivor, dispensing guidance, wisdom and advice to my fellow suffer-ers," he explained. Stonemason Peter moved his stones.

For some real victims, making lemonade out of lemons comes natu-rally. Someone steals the car? "At least my daughter wasn't in it." A hur-ricane blows the roof off? "We were lucky. We could have been killed." Surgery removes a tumor? "I just feel sorry for people whose tumors can't be removed."

From the Terezin concentration camp came…a cookbook. What's so special about a cookbook? Hey, this was a concentration camp, where there was no food. And the recipes, written in assorted hands, were for fancy dishes. The recipe book was a symbol that even in their darkest hour, these people clung to normalcy. They refused to be victims. They recast themselves.

Exercise:

In the previous chapter, you listed all the times you recall being a victim. For each one, recast yourself as the victor, as the person who survived, even conquered, rather than as the person who suffered. If you list an event so traumatic that you simply cannot recast yourself, search for meaning in the event—a reason why the event might create some good.

You might recall the famous World War II exotic dancer Mata Hari, who was charged with being a spy. On the way to her execution, she saw the crowd awaiting her. "All these people!" she declared. "What a success!"

Who runs your life? The victim gives control to other people. The victor charts his own course. That course almost inevitably leads up his Stairway to Heaven.

As a victor, you grip your sword by the handle high in the air. Aha! As a victim, you grasp your sword by the blade. **OUCH!** Don't do that. It hurts.

The importance of cheering EVERY success

Believing in herself, she never let them bring her down.
Now they'll proudly tell you this was her hometown.

—singer Lee Ann Womack in "Out of the Ordinary"

When your mood rises, you see the world through rose colored glasses. The more often your mood rises, the happier you feel, not just about the moment but about your life in general. Remember in Chapter 3 discussing why habits are so useful? So it is important to throw a parade for as many successes as possible, no matter how small. Make throwing a parade a habit.

Even after a setback, it's important to throw a parade. Researchers presented negative feedback to students on an alleged IQ test. That feedback led them to ruminate, to brood. But when given the chance to self-affirm after hearing the bad news, they ruminated much less. Reality is complicated. The spin we put on our stories governs how we think of ourselves.

When you were young, praise was your middle name. You were proud the first time you tied your shoelace. You were proud the first time you drew a house (even if nobody knew that's what it was). You were proud the first time you walked to school or slept over at a friend's house.

A story comes down of Angela, a mid-western veterinarian who brought her four-year-old son, Nicholas, to work with her. Like mother, like son: what she did to the animals, he did to his stuffed penguin toy. While Angela was busy with an old collie, the dog's owner remarked to Nicholas, "You're quite the vet-in-training. Maybe someday you'll be as good as your Mom." Nicholas looked up and replied, "I already am. See? The penguin feels better now." And he went back to the job of caring for his toy. To a child, anything can be a success.

I remember roaming through a modern art gallery, impressed by how…uh…modern the "art" was. At one point, I overheard a child of about seven vocalize what surely everyone in the gallery must have been thinking: "I could do that."

As adults, we no longer think about the thousands of things we do successfully each day. We take them for granted. We expect to do them well, so we don't give ourselves credit.

Exercise:

Earlier in this chapter, I asked you to write a list of all your accomplishments. It might have been easy for you to list a few major accomplishments, but what about all those little successes that add up to a happy life? If it helps, write down each success as it happens. Deposit them in a success bank. That's how some people keep perspective. In Chapter 3 we learned that thrills might be exciting, but chronic happiness lasts. The ingredients for chronic happiness are the thousands of little successes we cheer.

Another way to fire up the parade is to ask yourself, "Did I show up?" Life is not just about walking away with gold medals. As Woody Allen said, "Eighty percent of success is showing up." If you play the game of life, win or lose, you win. When you show up, plan for the best. Be optimistic. Feel lucky. Then look for what goes right and celebrate it.

You might want to know which comes first, believing in luck or happiness? Which comes first, positive illusions or happiness? Optimism or happiness? Success or happiness?

In most cases, happiness is both the result and the cause of so many factors. In other words, if you fake the nine habits of maximum happiness, you can boost your true happiness. The one thing you cannot fake is spirituality. You can stimulate your spirituality, you can explore it, but your beliefs and values must grow from within. However, the habits in this book can be forced if necessary; after a while, they become real, and you are happier. I've done it, I've felt it, and we'll discuss in a later chapter how you can, too.

So be a yayist and create those positive illusions. List your weekly, daily, hourly successes. Say them out loud. Strike up the band, and proclaim your victories. Pound on the drum. Toot the horn. You are the victor. Hip hip hooray! Celebrate your success, and move those stones. Climb your Stairway to Heaven.

HABIT # 2

Distinguish yourself

If the best man's faults were written on his forehead,
it would make him pull his hat over his eyes.

—Gaelic proverb

When we distinguish between two people, we recognize their differences. When someone is distinguished, we recognize his value. If you seek maximum happiness, you must feel unique, that you are your own person, that you are an individual. Clones need not apply.

As a unique individual, you need also to feel your own value. Adolph Hitler and Idi Amin were unique, thank goodness, but they had nothing to be proud of. They were not happy men. Mohandas Ghandi and Florence Nightingale were unique, and they had every reason to be happy about their uniqueness.

History abounds with tales of uniqueness: the warrior who's clever strategy defeats his evil foes, the inventor who's unorthodox ideas makes the breakthrough discovery, the artist who breaks from the pack and defines a new style. But history also shows that people remain social animals in search of similarity. We follow trends, we dress in current fashion, we adorn our homes in a similar manner. We seek common ground for bonding.

We define ourselves equally by what we are and by what we are not. By whom we associate with and by whom we avoid. By how we resemble others and by how we differ. We avoid standing out like the peacock or the flamingo, lest we feel like outcasts. On the other hand, our identity thrives on being recognizable from the swallows and finches and sparrows and warblers around us. We tend to emulate the cardinal or blue jay. In this tug-of-war, most people seek comfort in the middle ground.

What happens if you become very different, very unique, and very eccentric? People might look at you funny. But eccentrics—at least, *harmless* eccentrics—feel just as happy as you and I, if not more so. In fact, their uniqueness makes it easier to climb their Stairway to Heaven and see past the Great Wall of Misery.

Let's distinguish harmless eccentrics from deviants. Eccentrics are the company they keep, and they are in good company. They go their own way, but they don't wish others harm. They deviate in style, but not in their morals and values. Deviants, such as serial killers, rapists, and racists, eschew society's morals and values. Deviants are not happy.

Habit #2 does not suggest you become an eccentric (unless, of course, that's your goal) and certainly not a deviant. It simply advises you to place a high value on your own uniqueness. Habit #2 calls on you to distinguish yourself.

CHAPTER 6

Who paints your portrait?

If all pulled in the same direction, the world would keel over.

—Yiddish proverb

Portraits reveal a lot about their subjects' personalities. They also reveal a great deal about the painter. Let's ask ourselves, "Who paints our portrait?" Do you paint yours? Or do you let others paint it for you? We asked a similar question in Habit #1. We asked who controls your life. We asked if you play the victim by letting others control what you do and what happens to you. Or do you control your life? Those questions were about what you do. The questions in this chapter are about who you are.

Everybody wants to fit in, to relate to others, to be accepted. Everybody wants to...but some people need to. The problem is that human beings are more than just cardboard cutouts. When we rely on someone else's approval, we forfeit control of our happiness. We hide behind the Mask of Success in fear of disapproval. And fear does not mix well with happiness.

∞ *Peer pressure* ∞

This above all, to thine own self be true.

—Polonius in Hamlet, by William Shakespeare

One study found that HIV-infected gay men who try to keep their sexual orientation secret develop AIDS and die much faster than those who are open about their homosexuality. Another study shows how women who self-objectify or "adopt observers' perspectives on their physical selves" eat poorly and struggle more with math questions.

When we view ourselves through others' eyes, we let someone else paint our portraits. And when we imagine those eyes to be critical, we see ourselves not as Mona Lisa, but as one of Picasso's most distorted images. Not a pretty picture. Yale researchers found that even a bad hair day inspires feelings of incompetence and self-doubt.

Virginian Lori Charnee, whose family came to America from the Ukraine, describes the pressures that led her to anorexia: "The biggest pressure I felt was that the family sacrificed everything to come here. You feel like you need to make something of yourself. You are expected to succeed and pay back and be perfect."

I was privy to a speech by a student visiting from Japan. She described her frustration with Japan's highly conformist society. She explained how young people with no companion on Christmas or Valentines Day are treated as outcasts. She described the ritual of "obligation chocolates" that ladies must buy for male coworkers on Valentines Day. Throughout her speech, she kept referring to an old Japanese proverb: "The nail that sticks up gets pounded down."

Sometimes we fear that if we stick up or stick out, we will be pounded down. We cower in the shadow of society's hammer, ever fearful of the big bang. If we crouch low enough, maybe the hammer won't pound us down. We pay too much attention to the opinions others have of us.

Consider poor Tiger. After years of terrorizing the countryside, hunting deer, poaching livestock, killing game, Tiger grew long in the tooth. Finally, he knew it was time to retire. So he packed his bag and ambled into town to the Three Little Pigs Retirement Home Inc. He rang the bell, and the first little pig appeared on the landing above. "What do you want?" asked the little pig.

"I come here to retire," Tiger replied.

"Ooooh. I don't think so," the little pig declared. "You're not like us. You've got big teeth. Very dangerous. We can't let you in."

So Tiger went to the dentist and had his teeth removed. The next day, he returned to the Three Little Pigs Retirement Home Inc. "What do you want?" asked the second little pig.

"I have no more teeth. I come here to retire," Tiger replied once more.

"Ooooh. No, no, no. That just won't do," the little pig exclaimed. "You're different. You have sharp claws. You scare us. We can't let you in."

So Tiger went to the manicurist and had his claws removed. The next day, he returned to the Three Little Pigs Retirement Home Inc. "What do you want?" demanded the third little pig.

"I have no more claws. I come here to retire," Tiger repeated.

"Ooooh. Let me see," the little pig muttered as he disappeared from sight. Tiger heard much whispering and commotion behind the big wooden doors. "Okay, come in," said the little pig.

Tiger strolled through the doors, and there stood the three little pigs, grinning ear to ear. Suddenly they jumped on Tiger. Squealing with delight, they beat him up and sent him packing. No teeth. No claws. Yippeeee! Finally they got even with Tiger for terrorizing the animals.

Tiger should have known better. He should have accepted who he is and not try to conform to someone else's image of him. What tiger in his right mind lets a pig paint his portrait?

So where does our image come from? Who paints our portrait?

∞ *Life in Mediadom* ∞

It's amazing what a little makeup and photo retouching can do.
I hope it makes you feel better measuring up to us models,
because most of the look comes straight out of a bottle.

—model Tyra Banks

The media's paintbrush creates images of what we should be. And far too often, we try to fit the media's portrait instead of painting our own. Never underestimate the media battalions. We live in Mediadom.

A BBC documentary in 1966—an April Fool's Day prank, actually–tricked people into believing that farmers pick spaghetti from the vine. British viewers accepted the good news that Italian spaghetti farmers had overcome the ravages of the destructive spaghetti weevil.

If you doubt the power of the media, ask yourself what Eve gave to Adam. An apple, right? No. She tempted him with the "fruit" of the tree. Apples don't grow in the biblical climate. A fig or olive or grape would be more likely. Perhaps she tempted him with a date. But in Mediadom it's an apple, and that's what most people believe.

With that kind of power, consider the messages we get from the media:
- Studies show that the more time a person spends watching television, the more she perceives the world as it is portrayed on television.
- Not surprisingly, studies also show that soap opera fans have lower self-esteem, poorer coping, and less happiness.
- Planned Parenthood attributes today's high rates of teenage pregnancies and premarital sex to how sex is portrayed as a casual heat of the moment affair on television. In one soap opera season, for

example, unmarried partners hop in bed 24 times more frequently than married couples.
- Music packaged by the likes of the Spice Girls and Britney Spears teaches children to dress like harlots. When the media tells the kids that sex is for them, is it any wonder that teen pregnancies are on the rise? At their impressionable age, the media paints their portraits.
- Actress Susan Sarandon reflects on the film *Saving Private Ryan*, "That film tells you, basically… 'You want to be a guy, you have to kill at point-blank range. You're a hero.'"

The media creates more than just poor values and silly needs; it creates unrealistic expectations. Advertising warns us of all the things we simply cannot do without, all the things we deserve, all the things that EVERYBODY ELSE has. Sitcoms trick us into believing we can solve all our problems in 22 minutes flat. Soap operas teach us that adultery and manipulation are normal (and that sex is casual and that pregnancy is…wait a minute, what's pregnancy?). Newscasts panic us with images of violence everywhere. Movies deliver a worry-free world where nobody has to wear seat belts or condoms—a world where whatever we feel like doing at the moment is right, regardless of whom we hurt. All these media forms paint a picture of how we should look. And, with the exception perhaps of Danny DeVito, the Mediadom image is tall, half-naked, and anorexic.

POP QUIZ:
Can advertising affect our happiness?
ANSWER: Yes. Advertising hits us more frequently (some 3,000 times per day, 50 to 100 times before 9 a.m.) and more convincingly than ever before. Ads combine the power of the media's brush with the calculated agenda of manipulating us.

The very concept behind advertising, brands, positioning, marketing, etc. is to make us feel inadequate unless we buy the product. This works on all of us, but it works especially well on today's teenagers and children—I call them the Credit Card Kids—whose emotional and psychological skills are still being honed.

Advertising images are quick, upbeat, targeted. So are music videos and, increasingly, movies. No balance there. The Merchants of Misery create the most seductive images possible, but who can offer a counterpoint? It's all Ooh-la-la, without the blah-blah-blah. Who is there to point out that, "Yeah, it might be cool to have some of that stuff, but we're destroying the planet by over-consuming"? Who's there to say, "Hold on. Do I really need some multimillionaire's signature on my t-shirt or sneakers or golf shirt to feel like a worthy human being?"

Heroes and villains

After mass consumer culture stole our sense of individual identity, we all began looking for it in the human emblems of that very culture, its celebrities.

—Toronto journalist Leah McLaren

We watch pop divas, basketball players, and movie stars living *la vida loca*. We assume their glamorous adventures make them happy. We envy their presumably fulfilling lives. What a silly mistake. When people first discovered large dinosaur bones some 150 years ago, they assumed these were the bones of giants. Let's avoid the trap of assuming that some people are larger than life; appearances can be deceptive.

POP QUIZ:
If you met your reputation on the street, would you recognize each other?

Lots of people are not what they are cracked up to be. Americans revere John James Audubon as the father of American wildlife conservation. But in reality, he shot as many as 100 birds a day to get close enough to paint them in detail. Captain Bligh is usually portrayed as the villain in *Mutiny on the Bounty*, but he was, in fact, a most caring captain who even allowed wet sailors to dry off in his cabin. And hyenas are scavengers, right? Well, actually, it's often the lions that scavenge the hyenas' prey.

Will we ever learn? One celebrity exposé after another reveals misery, drugs, alcohol, abuse, fear. Yet we still believe. When singer Janis Joplin clutched the microphone, reports one biographer, she "was no longer fat, ratty-haired, bad-complexioned; she was the leading lady, both wanted and adored. Offstage she had whisky and heroine to comfort her."

During the Persian Gulf War, we saw a comic sign of just how strong the notion of celebrity has become. Baghdad Betty broadcast over Iraqi radio: "GI, you should be home. While you're away, movie stars are taking your women. Robert Redford is dating your girlfriend. Tom Selleck is kissing your lady. Bart Simpson is making love to your wife." Nice touch, Betty.

Celebrities are the gods and goddesses of Mediadom. People have always looked up to their heroes, and heroes make great role models. But celebrities can't always make the same claim. Fits of rage, divorces, adultery, even biting off another person's ear; these are hardly ideal examples to follow. However, some celebrities make great role models. Jane Goodall, Christopher Reeve, Mother Teresa, and Terry Fox spring to mind.

Happiness researcher David Lykken, Ph.D., points out, "Only members of our species develop a detailed mental picture of ourselves and of our attitudes, a self-concept." He explains that, since we tend to evaluate others, having a self-concept means making comparisons with people we admire or disdain.

POP QUIZ:

Which of the following six celebrities should you compare yourself to?

• Colin Powell
• Martina Navratilova
• Janet Jackson
• Howard Stern
• Tiger Woods
• Jennifer Aniston

ANSWER: If you want maximum happiness, try comparing yourself to Howard Stern. Why? Because very few Americans hold a positive image of him, according to a Gallop poll. What do you think? Can you measure up to him? See, doesn't that make you feel better already? That's one way for you to move the stones. But if you compare yourself unfavorably to those few people you see at the pinnacle of greatness, don't expect to be very pleased with yourself.

⊗ *Nastymirrorosis* ⊗

Mirror, Mirror on the wall,
who's the fairest of them all?

—the Queen to her mirror in *Snow White*

Fashion writer Tralee Pearce writes about skin color, "It is the primal fear of the pale-skinned woman embarking on a tropical vacation. No matter how buff her buttocks, nor how chic her bikini, the prospect of a horrid day-one display of Casper-the-Ghost pallor is enough to keep her on the wrong side of the hotel room door indefinitely." Pop goes the ego!

Wait a minute. Why would a person be so afraid of how other people see her skin that she would deprive herself of pleasure? Who set this standard anyway? It seems that Coco Chanel, after World War I, first promoted tanned skin to match her style of designer dresses. So why persist in trying to look the way this woman wanted people to in such ancient times? And why feel inferior if you don't ?

Millions of women stare into the mirror, inflated physically but deflated emotionally. They suffer from nastymirrorosis (another great Dictionary of David word). Higher body weight is associated with increased depression and suicide in women. In men, suicide and depression relate more to lower body weight. These people, men and women alike, would be better off to focus on growing happier.

Meg Kennedy explains, "It turned out that weight was a symptom, not a cause. I'm not happier because I lost 30 pounds, but I was able to lose 30 pounds because I'm happier." It's hard to be a yayist when searching for faults.

Time for a reality check. Most physical features, including some of our weight, are foundation stones. They cannot be moved. I am often tempted to be a few inches taller, but my reality check frowns on this. I have to decide whether to be miserable over the inches I don't have or happy with those I do. Yes, I choose happiness.

A now-smaller Catherine McGravey reflects on her overweight past: "It made me not only a victim, but also a participant in my own victim-ization.... My obesity defined who I was, not only to those prejudiced and of narrow mind but, more importantly, to myself." When you see things that lead you to feel small, that make you feel worthless, that evoke a sense of failure, that's when you know the mirror hangs on a stone in the Great Wall of Misery. You're the stonemason, remember? Move your multiple-choice stones to your Stairway to Heaven, and climb on top of them. Catherine moved hers.

Why are 85 percent of women not satisfied with their bodies? Why does an entire industry cater to body image obsession or help women exercise girth control? Training. Women have been trained to relate their self-worth to their physical appearance and, particularly, to their weight. Advertising. Films. Television. Fashion. What Joni Mitchell dubbed "the star-maker machinery" barely tolerates "normal" people, let alone plus-size customers.

The ultimate guidebook for an aspiring actress, pop singer, or model would be titled *How to toothpickify yourself on two-and-a-half calories a week.* Over the past 80 years, Miss America pageant winners have grown 2 percent taller and 12 percent lighter, so that many of them now fit the World Health Organization's definition of under-nutrition.

Like hamburgers on the grill, teenage girls feel the heat and the pressure to squeeze every last ounce of fat from their bodies. If Claudia Schiffer can look so thin, so must they. If Naomi Campbell can be that slender, they can, too. Why not?

Girls are taught from their earliest days playing with Barbie® dolls. In human terms, her measurements would be an incredible 39-21-33 (but still a little stiff to cuddle with). Or, as humorist Erma Bombeck put it, "(Barbie®) looks like she just whipped through puberty in fifteen minutes."

A mother-daughter study shows how lower-weight university-aged daughters have higher levels of body weight surveillance and body shame than their heavier mothers do. With all the false expectations we thrust at them, it's no wonder young ladies struggle with anorexia and bulimia more than ever before. If you try to fit a size 14 reality into size 4 expectations, you're bound to be disappointed. That's the law of physiques.

Attempts to create the ideal human, with no room for flaws, eccentricity, or uniqueness, can inflict disaster...and not just for your personal happiness. Adolf Hitler built his Arian nation on that principle and set about eradicating anyone labelled "undesirable." In their quest for Utopia, the early Communists devastated families, churches, and the environment. Religious fundamentalist societies often persecute and torture those who insist on remaining imperfect.

If, at any time, you feel inclined to think there is such a thing as an ideal physique, watch the movies *Moonraker* or *Gattica*. Or consider this short letter from young Norma: "Dear God: Did you mean for the giraffe to look like that or was it an accident?" Of course, we all look different. That's how we're supposed to look. Each of us is unique.

Speaking of giraffes and models, I recall a conference where I took in an early breakfast so as to get some pre-meeting work done. I headed up to the floor where breakfast was to be served, and, as the elevator doors opened, I stepped out onto an alien planet—the Planet of the FlagPole Damsels! Dozens of them. Every one at least six feet tall. Every one at most a size four. Every one just hanging out, listless, not talking, and not having anywhere to go. I've always been a *Star Trek* fan, but this was just too spooky. Surely I had landed on the wrong floor. But I soon discovered I was on the right floor. I looked more closely at the conference program and realized a fashion show was scheduled during breakfast later on, and the FlagPole Damsels were to be the models.

Having myself escaped from the Planet of the FlagPole Damsels, I can warn you. If ever you thought, even just for a moment, "Gee, I sure wish I could look more like those gorgeous models on the Paris and Milan runways," stop right now. Trust me, you do not really want to look like them. We men need more than human hangers to snuggle with. Skin and bones are not enough!

On the other hand, if you are genuinely and truly overweight, by all means, lose the extra pounds. But please do it for your health, not for your self-worth. The same goes if you are underweight. Thin or fat, we are worth no more and no less than we believe we are. Let's teach ourselves to revel in who we are the way we are. Nastymirrorosis can be cured. I know that is far from easy for some people, but it's the price of happiness. And it's worth it. You are worth it.

Just who do you think you are?

Learning to love yourself is the greatest love of all.

—singer Whitney Houston in "The Greatest Love of All"

Farmer Brown is trying to paint Sarah Sheep's and Bray Goat's portraits. He's painting them as losers, as has-beens, as worthless. Imagine if Sarah Sheep and Bray Goat allow nastymirrorosis to take over. At this moment they look ragged, covered in bruises, drained of energy, and above their heads old Farmer Brown keeps dumping stones down the well. They have to believe they are worth every effort it takes to shake the stones off and step up. Shake the stones off and step up. Shake the stones off…

Paula Lingo was a nastymirrorosis sufferer, but she managed to move her stones. "Other people saw a gutsy woman, mother of five, working two jobs, always smiling, never tired, and positive that each day would be better. Employers praised me. Strangers complimented me and became friends. Men found me attractive and witty. My mirror couldn't see this. Instead, staring at me was a dumb blond. I was too tall, too fat, no personality, and a crooked mouth with a lopsided smile…. One day I looked in the mirror and liked what I saw. Looking back at me was a tall attractive blond. She still had a crooked mouth and smile, but now it was unique." Why do so many mirrors make Mona Lisa look and feel like a Picasso distortion?

A wise Toastmaster I know told me that "what you think of me is none of my business." (I had to stop to think about that one.) She then proceeded to unshackle her hair from the fake color she had been applying for over a decade. She had started dying her hair early, in response to "millions, maybe billions of dollars" of advertising. The Merchants of Misery strike again! Apparently, women use an average of 21 products each day to make themselves look better. (And presumably more natural?)

Beauty is only skin deep. But happiness builds from within. That's why it is so important to paint our own portrait and not let television, friends, celebrities, or the Merchants of Misery paint it for us.

CHAPTER 7

Shine like a diamond

Every bee's honey is sweet.

—French proverb

Like a skillfully cut diamond, you are unique. You are a rare gem. Go ahead and shine. Be proud of everything that is unique about you. And what might that be?

Your background is unique. Nobody shares your family, your experiences, your homes, your thoughts. Nobody, that is, except you. Rubin "Hurricane" Carter describes what it's like to be locked away for 20 years: "You are confronted with yourself, because that's all you have to deal with: is self, you."

Your identity is unique. When your name is called, your telephone number dialed, your e-mail address connected, or your photograph shown, you know it's you and nobody else. You might even wince if someone misspells or mispronounces your name. On the wall across the room is a Pennsylvania license plate my friend, Mark,

made for me. Across the top is written, "Save Wild Animals." Across the middle is written simply "DAVID." That's my wall. That's my name (although I'm not sure I'm a wild animal).

Your fingerprints are unique. Your DNA and dental records, too. According to police in Michigan and a Judge in Washington State, ear prints now are also unique.

Your face is unique. You might object to being mistaken for someone else. A police composite sketch of Pittsburgh's East End Rapist bore an uncanny resemblance to both Minnesota Vikings Quarterback Daunte Culpepper and Houston Rockets Forward Charles Barkley. I'm sure they were not pleased to see the three photos published side by side in the newspaper.

Your mind is unique. Your thoughts, dreams, fears, goals, philosophy, values, and traditions are yours and yours alone. If I could tailor this book just for you, I would draw examples from your unique experiences and focus on your unique goals and dreams. But since I'm hoping six billion people will read this book, optimist that I am, I have to generalize just a bit.

Shining like a diamond is about more than just being proud of the differences we're stuck with. It means feeling free to be different in ways we might be shy to right now. Let's proudly act different when we get the urge to. In fact, it is downright good to be

What's in a name?

Imagine how shocked I was when my brother showed me my byline on an article I never wrote. It seems a *New York Times* business reporter shares my rather unique name. Hey! That's **my** name!

different if something in your surroundings is cruel or hurtful. Better to use less wasteful packaging when others are double-bagging, to smile when others are waving their fists, to share when others are hoarding. As novelist Lillian Hellman said, "I will not cut my conscience to fit this year's fashions."

Happiness means setting your own standards and following your own heart and making up your own mind, not deferring to others' standards and satisfying their visions. Describing the dark years of communism in his country, Czechoslovakia's post-Communist President Vaclav Havel said, "We fell morally ill because we became used to saying something different than what we thought."

The Berlin Wall was the Great Wall of Misery for millions of people. One day, the shear force of free will sent the stones tumbling to the ground. Vaclav Havel helped place those stones on the Stairway to Heaven.

Abraham Lincoln was also a shining diamond. A foreign diplomat walked in on him one day while he was polishing his boots. The diplomat exclaimed, "What, Mr. President, you black your own boots?" Lincoln answered, "Yes." Then he added, "Whose do you black?" He shone even more than his boots.

∞ *Eccentrics shine* ∞

Nobody can be just like me.
Sometimes even I have trouble doing it.

—actress Tallulah Bankhead

Eccentrics shine brightest of all. This does not mean we have to become a hermit, wage a crusade against a cactus needle conspiracy, or plaster our walls with junk mail. It does mean that we could learn something about being happy from those who do.

"Eccentricity is at least partly a matter of choice, a choice that usually requires considerable bravery," says neuro-psychologist David Weeks, the world's foremost expert on eccentricity.

CASE: Doctor Patch Adams dresses as a clown when visiting patients. He pooh-poohs the notion common in medical practice that patients prefer doctors with a serious bearing. He believes humor is integral to healing and is not afraid to show it. He was the subject of a touching movie.

CASE: Barbara Silburt collects junk. In her own words, "Worse, not only do I obsessively squirrel away all of my own junk, I'll eagerly take in yours, too. And, unlike many collectors, who specialize in certain kinds of junk, I'm an omnivore." (Memo to my Dad: You've been upstaged. Saving old newspapers, egg cartons, and cereal boxes is bush league.) Barbara is clearly happy, reveling in both preserving the environment and in tasting another era.

CASE: Nikola Tesla, famous electrical inventor, had columbiphilia (love of pigeons), scotophilia (love of the dark) and triphilia (obsession with the number 3). He often signed his letters "G.I.," for Great Inventor.

CASE: An anonymous New York City man operates an Apology Line telephone service for anyone who wants to express regret or listen to the *mea culpas* of others. To fund the project, he sells a "Greatest Hits" tape.

CASE: Nick Nolte, famous actor, sometimes wears bathrobes to film premieres and sits in blue-striped pajamas for a magazine interview.

CASE: Kentucky artists, Bud and Bert, build custom coffins for an eccentric clientele. Their artwork includes an Easter egg pattern, a steamship (in 3-D) with dual smokestacks, and a dog-themed urn for Oscar the dog, of Oakland, California.

CASE: I see Arlene Lambert drive around Toronto with hundreds of plastic dolls glued to her car. It's really quite a sight to see.

CASE: Chief Siloh, a native of London, England, wears the full dress costume of a Cherokee chief.

CASE: Edward Leedskalnin, the rock man from Florida, secretly sculpted a rock garden: 12 rocking chairs, beds, and cradles; a 25-foot tall obelisk; planets; a map of Florida; and a giant wall around his property. The nine-ton coral rock gate opens at the touch of a finger. Most amazing was how he calculated the point on which the huge stone had to pivot and how he moved all the giant stones by himself. (Do I have to add that Edward moved his stones?)

CASE: Francis Galton, anthropologist and prolific author of more than 300 publications, was obsessed with measuring and counting everything: the curves on a woman's body, the number of brush strokes to paint a portrait, even the length of rope necessary to break a criminal's neck without dropping the head.

What do all these eccentrics have in common? According to Dr. Weeks, eccentrics are nonconforming, creative, curious, idealistic, happily obsessed, aware of being different since childhood, intelligent, opinionated, noncompetitive, not interested in reassurance from others, unusual in eating and living habits, unsociable, single, enjoy a mischievous sense of humor, usually the eldest or an only child, and a poor speller.

Their happiness is because most eccentrics do not depend on reassurance from others. The Merchants of Misery can't trick them. They choose to do what pleases them and to enjoy it. So there! They ignore the dew stones and place the multiple-choice stones where they wish. In some ways, eccentrics are an exaggeration of what everybody wants to be but is afraid to try.

Eccentricity is not everybody's medicine. Compromises between who we are and what others expect allow us to function within society. For example, I wear a tie. Do I do this because I am enamored with ties? Definitely not! Surely, ties are a plot by women seeking revenge for high heels. (I don't blame them, but high heels are not my fault.) Nevertheless, I wear a tie because it's part of the costume required to "fit in" enough for me to play a constructive leadership role in society. On the other hand, many of my ties reflect my identity, featuring wildlife, license plates, and happiness.

But doesn't wearing a tie against my own preference mean I'm caving in to peer pressure? Well, a tie is just a piece of cloth. I might dislike it, but I'm not compromising my values, my interests, my ideas, or anything meaningful. What can be less meaningful than a tie? That's the difference between simply being sociably unique and being eccentric; the eccentric doesn't care to make even the small compromises that allow him to fully participate in society.

∞ *Are you a human doing?* ∞

All the stuff our parents told us didn't come true.
No one cares if you're good.
People only care if you're good looking or rich.

—television executive Rosalyn Weinman

John Wareham, a prominent corporate headhunter, says, "To be a great executive you have to become a great person, and the way to do this is to follow your own personal goals—not somebody else's." He counsels that not everyone is a leader and that you might in fact be happier not to "go against the emotional grain" by taking on a leadership role not suited to your temperament. In other words, the career ladder does not necessarily help you scale the wall. It depends on your unique set of goals, values, and personality traits.

I rejoiced in a letter to the editor from bank manager Rae Benjamin. He wrote about his son, who works with his hands. He wrote about how he is urging his son to value the manual labor he clearly loves—that it is "just as useful to society if he puts in an honest day's work using his hands as he would be if he had a hundred degrees." He supports his son's uniqueness and shines like a diamond.

As a campaign manager for a candidate in a national election, I learned that each person brings his unique contribution, his own insecurities, and his personal motivation. To run a successful campaign, each person must be given the chance to shine, to feel he is contributing, to know his time and his effort is somehow an investment not an expenditure.

You and I are human beings, not human doings. Our behavior alone is not our identity. Okay, so this might seem obvious, but most people don't think this way. When we meet someone new, one of the first questions we face is, "What do you do?" How do you answer? I raise my kids? I camp? I enjoy adventure novels? Or do you answer that you're a librarian, financial advisor, bus driver, nurse, Web page designer, sales representative, post-industrial nuclear micro-biologist, or whatever you do to put bread on the table? Perhaps we try to hide behind the Mask of Success. Are you what you do, or are you what you think, how you feel, what you believe?

Who am I? My bio sheet says I'm a consumer advocate and a speaker and a community participant and a husband. I like to think of myself as a well-rounded person, but, as with so many people, I have to admit that I let my work define me more than it should.

Exercise:

Think up two good answers to "What do you do?" that you can use without mentioning something that involves salary or career.

Be a human being, not just a human doing.

∞ *Be who you are!* ∞

I didn't pay any attention when everyone told me I should get a real job.
I love performing.

—Broadway chorus dancer Paula Giffin

Painter Pablo Picasso told this story: "My mother said to me, 'If you become a soldier, you'll be a general, if you become a monk, you'll end up as the Pope.' Instead, I became a painter and wound up as Picasso." Like his work or hate it, you have to admit that Picasso was not shy to be who he was.

POP QUIZ:
Which of the following describes Martha Stewart?

✘   Satanic slave driver, pressuring women to achieve perfection, crushing their egos and destroying their lives.

✔   Angelic heroine, forcing Wall Street to stand up and salute what was once disparagingly referred to as "woman's work."

Shining like a diamond means being proud of who we are, rather than relying on others to determine our value. There's no question that Martha Stewart has polished her diamonds, ignoring the naysayers and charging forward to her own rhythm.

Congresswoman Patricia Schroeder captured the essence of shining like a diamond when she described being one of only 14 women in Congress as "wearing a bathing suit in church—hard to miss."

Many women who've made it into male-dominated boardrooms have had to shine like a diamond to do so. Barbara Spector, a New York executive, found herself at a meeting with 11 male executives. Imagine how she felt when the meeting leader turned to her and said, "Sweetie, could you get us some coffee please?" Then again, can you imagine how the man next to her felt when she turned to him and whispered as loudly as possible, "I think he's talking to you."

In a similar vein, Kathie Lee Gifford stood up for herself when filling in for David Letterman. In mid-show, a bra landed on her lap, accompanied by the trumpeting cry of, "Put on a bra!" And that's just what she did...right then and there.

What's in a name?

When Marcia Kilgore was seeking a name for her spa, she asked herself, "What is the best possible feeling that someone could walk out of my salon with? Then came *Bliss!*"

Shining like a diamond is about being at ease with who you are and not changing just to please other people. After all, you can't forge your own signature. Sophia Loren understood. When asked why she attended so few parties, she replied, "The party is where I am." Meryl Streep said, "I have always regarded myself as the pillar of my life." These women have the guts to shine. Each one moved her stones.

Marcia Kilgore, the owner of BlissWorld, might seem like an unlikely candidate to shine like a diamond. Her official biography reads: "Unlike her model and movie star clients, Marcia's own skin was a bit on the 'wild' side." That didn't stop her from conquering the business world with her own spa and body products distribution business (focusing more on how clients *feel* than on how they *look*). Her success is based on street smarts, personality, and sheer determination.

Shining like a diamond is also the story of the ugly duckling, teased, tormented, led to believe he was less valuable than others, until one day his inner beauty blossomed. He was a swan, not a duck. When others see an ugly duckling in you—or when you *think* others see an ugly duckling—stand proud, like the swan that you are.

Dominic didn't seem too bright to the other kids at the playground. They would tease him by holding up a nickel and a dime and ask him which one he wants. "The big one," he would always say. The kids would laugh. One teacher had seen this happen a few times. She pulled Dominic aside one day and asked him, "Don't you know they're just making fun of you?" Dominic looked her in the eyes and said, "Of course. But if I picked the dime, how much longer would the fun continue?" They laugh, but Dominic is happy just shining brightly.

∽ S-nd yours-lf a m-ssag- ∽

Friendship with oneself is all-important,
because without it one cannot be friends with anyone else.

—First Lady Eleanor Roosevelt

Studies show that the only consistent predictor of a nation's happiness is its level of individualism. That was one of the great failures of communism. Ironically, it could be one of the great failures of world capitalism, too.

Everywhere around the world, uniqueness is under attack. As global brands are slowly taking over the international marketplace, as cookie cutter buildings replace local architecture, a world devoid of uniqueness can no longer be dismissed as a science fiction fantasy. *Brave New World* and *Logan's Run* might seem unreal, but the conformity they suggest is spreading across our little planet.

It sometimes feels like anyone trying to be a unique individual these days is an endangered species. Ironically, the Merchants of Misery, who monitor our pulse 24 hours a day, know how desperate we are to break free from the herd. They mass market clothing and other items that are fashionably unfashionable. Their double-talk advertising tells us to express our individuality by us all buying their product. They make the Credit Card Kids feel rebellious about feeding the corporate pinstripes.

Here's a yayist letter you might want to send yourself the next time you feel your individuality doesn't count:

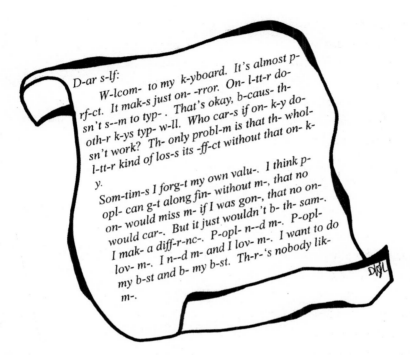

After all, are we not all made in God's image? Are we not all worth our weight in gold?

Do you remember ever saying to your parents or to your spouse or even to a friend, "Please love me the way I am." As the German philosopher Johann von Goethe said, "I am what I am, so take me as I am!"

Asking for unconditional love is, in fact, a request for the other person to be happy with you. Think about the black hole of distress you and that person feel when you do not accept each other the way you are. Now think about the bouquet of warmth you both feel when you do accept each other as you are. See? When one person accepts another person's uniqueness, it's all about sharing happiness. And can you think of a better gift to share?

Remember that scarcity increases value. A rare gem fetches a high price. "One of a kind" and "Hurry in while they last" are slogans that help sell otherwise unspectacular goods by making them appear to be rare gems. When we hear someone say, "You're one in a million," we know we've made a mark.

You can choose between being a priceless diamond or a worthless bauble. Diamonds are rare, and so they are precious. Baubles can be found on every street corner. Be unique. Be proud. Be a diamond. Then shine…because there is nobody just like you.

HABIT # 3

*I murmured because I had no shoes,
until I met a man who had no feet.*

—Persian proverb

Sarah Sheep stops abruptly. "Why me?" she asks herself. She wonders why nothing ever seems to go her way. Why is she stuck deep in a well with a silly old goat, while the rest of the world's sheep roam free? Why does she ache from crashing stones, when the rest of the world's sheep relax in their pastures? Why do so many sheep seem to have so much, when she has so little?

We ask ourselves the same question: why is the grass always greener on the other side of the fence? Actually, there's a logical reason, which we'll see shortly. The trick is not to glance over the fence. With ample grass on our side, we can roll in the joy of our own grass.

Meanwhile, Bray Goat has had about enough of the stones pummeling him. He wonders when it will stop. Will he ever feel safe? Will he ever enjoy peace and quiet? Will he ever graze on the Green Pastures of Cloud Nine? "Why me?" he wonders.

Far too often, we sit around waiting for our ship to come in, for Prince Charming to ride up, for the lottery's Big Yahoo. Another day passes, and we wait some more. Another day passes. One more day passes. And as each day passes, another tomorrow fades into yesterday. But chronic happiness feeds on the thousands of little gifts each day brings. At any one time, 1,800 thunderstorms rage somewhere in the world. There's really no point waiting for a sunny day to smile.

POP QUIZ:
Do orange and purple go well together?
ANSWER: Believe it or not, yes...when they combine to display a majestic sunset. So let's not take anything for granted. Let's enjoy the beauty around us.

Why not rejoice today in the abundance we have, instead of sitting in misery hoping that some outside force will bring us happiness? Don't wait another day. Habit # 3 calls on you to count your blessings.

CHAPTER 8

Great expectations

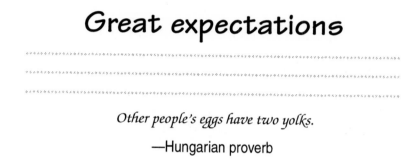

Other people's eggs have two yolks.

—Hungarian proverb

This is your lucky day. Actually every day is. How do I know? Because your unlucky day is when you dream you ate the world's biggest marshmallow, then wake and your pillow is…wait a minute! Where's your pillow? Or when you wonder why the apple juice tastes funny, just as your daughter calls out, "Have you seen my science project anywhere?"

Robert Garside has had his share of unlucky days. In his bid to be the first person to jog around the world, he was shot at in Russia, robbed in Pakistan, imprisoned in China, and threatened with guns and knives in Panama and Mexico. This is not your unlucky day.

This might seem like just an ordinary day to you. Did you expect better? How we feel depends on our expectations.

POP QUIZ:
Would you rather feel like this is your lucky day, or would you prefer to call it an ordinary day?

Like most people, you probably prefer this to feel like your lucky day. Actor-turned-producer Danny DeVito delights in finding camera angles to shoot movie scenes. What others in the film industry find tedious charges him up. That is just what this chapter and the next one will help you do—charge up on "ordinary" things. My, isn't this your lucky day!

Expectations smother joy

A great obstacle to happiness is to expect too much happiness.

—French scientist Bernard de Fontenelle

There is a difference between desire and expectation. We can desire to be healthy, for instance, or we can expect to be healthy. If we desire to be healthy, each day we wake up pleased to have what we desire. If we expect to be healthy, it's just not that exciting. Worse, if we fall sick, we feel cheated out of an entitlement.

Sickness is actually quite a useful dew stone. It helps us appreciate our health instead of expecting it. On his 75th birthday, Dick Shields, of Pittsburgh, reflected on his life, including a week-long, near-death coma; a broken neck (three times); triple bypass heart surgery; a blood vessel blockage bigger than a tennis ball; skinless feet (due to a fungus); and a broken back: "I'd have to say I've been truly blessed." And I'd have to say he *really* moved his stones.

Hunger makes us appreciate food, which I believe, in part, explains the Christian tradition of fasting for Lent and the Muslim tradition of fasting for Ramadan. Thirst teaches us to appreciate water. Fatigue helps us appreciate sleep.

On the other hand, we seldom appreciate what we have in abundance. Even I, who love cheesecake, stop appreciating it after the forty-third slice. But when it's been months since I've had a slice, there's little

I appreciate more. Our own expectations determine our appreciation, and we control our expectations.

How many people dream of living the tale of Snow White or Cinderella or Sleeping Beauty? That's the dream of "And they lived happily ever after..." But happily ever after doesn't reflect reality any more than the part about the evil stepsisters or the magic mirror (which is an extreme example of nastymirrorosis in action). What if you marry someone other than Prince Charming or Superman? What if he's a mere mortal?

Minnesota psychologist Ellen Berschei says, "If the inevitable odds against eternal passionate love in a relationship were better understood, more people might choose to be satisfied with the quieter feelings of satisfaction and contentment." She and her colleagues conclude that the growing divorce rate is due in part to unrealistic expectations about romance.

Christmastime also stirs romantic, nostalgic notions. Whatever your tradition, it probably includes wistfuller-than-life imagery. For many of us it is nevertheless a time of great joy. Family. Food. Gifts. Carols. Decorations. But for almost a third of us, it disappoints. Bickering. Jealousy. Torn dreams. We inflate our expectations of the holiday season. We expect perfection.

But the real world isn't perfect. The cousin who never liked you is not about to start just because it's Christmas. You won't suddenly warm up to a sibling's annoying habit just because it's Christmas. The holidays bear greater joy when wrapped in realistic expectations.

And then there are the gifts. A gift is something one person voluntarily gives another just because she feels like it. But Christmas gifts aren't usually like that. We give gifts to make others like us or because we're expected to. (Otherwise, why do all the gifts coincidentally show up at the same time—Christmas?). And we usually expect gifts in return, or we feel shunned, insulted, unappreciated. Expectations stifle satisfaction.

∽ *The age of entitlement* ∾

*The human race has had long experience
and a fine tradition in surviving adversity.
But we now face a task for which we have little experience,
the task of surviving prosperity.*

—pollster Alan Gregg

Okay, time to get controversial (again). Stop expecting Christmas gifts. I don't mean to refuse gifts. I don't mean to stop giving them if that brings you joy. Just stop expecting them. Stop feeling entitled. If you expect no gift, you cannot feel rejection. What a liberating sensation! And if you receive a gift, no matter how simple, you can be genuinely gratified and joyful.

POP QUIZ:
How much of a bonus do you think it takes to lift your spirits?
ANSWER: Not much. Psychologist Norbert Schwartz placed a dime on the office photocopy machine. After some users came and went, he placed a new dime. After others, he did not. He followed this up by interviewing all users about their lives. It turns out that those who found the extra change in their pockets wanted less change in their lives. All it took was a little bonus—a very little bonus—to make these people happier.

At a creative thinking workshop I attended, the trainers presented each of us with a parting gift...a clown nose. What a buoyant mood that simple bonus inspired, and it lingered in the hallways for the rest of the conference.

Your life is jam-packed with ordinary little things. How would you feel if—Presto!—you could turn them into bonuses?

I admit, it's hard to kill swollen expectations created by gazillions of dollars of advertising. The Merchants of Misery inflate our expectations. Let me give you an example of how advertising creates false expectations. A Maryland man approached pharmacist Catherine Cooke with a magazine ad that featured just the name of a drug and a snow-capped mountain. When she told him the ad was for an allergy medicine, and he did not have allergies, he was disappointed.

University of Toronto professor Nancy Howell identifies Mediadom's entitlement message as a reason so many well-off people can't seem to make ends meet. She says, "We're bombarded by advertisers who say we're not only entitled to every comfort, but we deserve it."

Psychotherapists often see patients who are convinced they've been cheated by life because they deserve better—even though they've got it pretty good.

Entitlement can also deter us from doing what would increase our happiness. This is the premise of the bestseller *Who Moved My Cheese?* by Spencer Johnson. There was no cheese left for Hem and Haw, but they felt entitled. Instead of looking for cheese elsewhere, they stubbornly waited for it to come to them…because they were entitled to it. Welcome to the age of entitlement, where instead of moving the multiple-choice stones, we stubbornly insist on being miserable.

Exercise:

Remember the list of things you feel you need that you prepared in Chapter 2? Take it out and look at each item. Take a few moments to appreciate them. Nothing on that list is a true necessity. Everything is a wonderful bonus you are lucky to have.

In Chapter 2, we learned how money does not buy happiness. One of the reasons is because expectations swell with income. We earn a raise at work, and instead of enjoying it as a bonus, we quickly start to expect it—to feel entitled to it. It ceases to be a source of joy and becomes simply another of the resources on which we rely.

I find fights over inheritance particularly sad. Inheritance is a gift, a bonus, not something we should expect. But how often, against our own best judgment perhaps, do we allow squabbles over our entitlement to mar our memory or destroy relationships? Would you rather feel entitled and miserable or grateful and happy?

∞ *Don't take things for granted* ∞

Most of the time, it's the new flames that shine.
When they'll leave you in the dark,
it's the gentle glow of family love
that can mend your broken heart.

—country band Farmer's Daughter in "Family Love"

When we feel entitled to something, we take it for granted. We set ourselves on autopilot and miss the joy we could experience from our everyday lives. Familiarity doesn't really breed contempt, just boredom. As the Sufi Caliph said when commanding pilgrims to leave Mecca quickly, "I fear if you grow too familiar with the Holy City, the awe of it will depart from your hearts."

This is similar to the spotmisserism we encountered in Chapter 4. Just as it is easy to overlook the frequent accomplishments we take for granted, we also often overlook the ample blessings we take for granted. We see only the things we don't have.

One risk of taking people for granted is that we might abandon those we need the most. That's because we undervalue what we take for granted, as typically happens when we meet a new flame. Suddenly this person is the world, and we seem to forget our family and friends. To some degree, that's good. We have to pay attention to a new romantic interest because that person might become the central person in our lives.

But we've all heard stories of people who abandon all their friends, even their family, for a new flame. They cut all ties. Like a camel that's just undergone a humpectomy, they leave themselves without support. That is not healthy. We need a variety of relationships, and we must never undervalue those people who stick by us when we are most in need.

⊂∞⊃ *The grass is always greener* ⊂∞⊃

The world can be a horrible, cruel place—
and at the same time it can be an abundant, wonderful place.
These are both truths.

—Stanford University psychologist Lee Ross

POP QUIZ:
Is the grass always greener on the other side of the fence?
ANSWER: Yes, but it's an optical illusion. Look over at your neighbor's yard. The grass is greener, and there's a good reason. Look down at the grass between your feet. From this angle, you see each blade as not much more than a dot, and you see the brown earth between the blades. Now look across at your neighbor's lawn. You see the blades from the side, and they cover up the brown earth between them. (And for this illusion we spray poison all over our lawns?)

Life is full of illusions. *They* always seem to be more organized than we are. *They* never fight. *His* wife is prettier. *Her* husband takes out the trash. *They* can afford a third car. Just who are "they," anyway? They are anyone with something we don't have. It's sometimes easy to forget that we all have things. We have some they don't have, and naturally they have some we don't. That's the way it should be. We are all different (remember to celebrate your own uniqueness?), so we all have different things.

As we explored in previous chapters, expectations often arise from comparisons with others. Comparisons with those who are better off—or seem to be better off—plague us with expectationmania. If our neighbor has it all, we reason, why can't we? Yes, that's it. We, too, must have it all! So here we stand in the Land of Plenty, bemoaning the things we lack, rather than being pleased with all we have.

Alas, we rarely compare ourselves with people less well off. Even the rich fall prey to harmful comparisons (like every time a baseball or basketball contract comes up for negotiation). Envious people are never happy. They cannot enjoy what they have, and they are upset with what others have.

Truthfully, when we say, "I can't afford that," we really mean, "I choose to spend my money on more important things."

Of course, some things we all need: food, water, shelter, affection. But much of what we want is not that necessary. When we feel entitled to those things, it's more greed than need.

Our grass really is pretty green already. All we need to make our lawns the Green Pastures of Cloud Nine is to appreciate the green grass we have.

∞ *Want what you have* ∞

Now I know we had no money, but I was rich as I could be,
In that coat of many colors, my Momma made for me.

—singer Dolly Parton in "Coat of Many Colors".

In the contest between need and greed, need will always be satisfied first. Our goal should be to satisfy needs, and enjoy them. Yayists want what they have. But greed feeds on fairy tale expectations that will never be satisfied. When we surrender to greed's expectations, we lock ourselves into a cage of misery.

In their quest for maximum happiness, Buddhists rid themselves of desire. They reason that if one desires what he doesn't have, he cannot be happy. But if one has no desires, he cannot be disappointed.

For our purposes, let's just not desire things we cannot have. Let's want the things we have instead of frustrating ourselves over the things we want. If we want what we have, we find all the happiness in the world in our own hands—or more correctly, in our hearts, where happiness has to begin.

You might recall the song "One Tin Soldier" by Coven. A treasure lies buried beneath the stone in the mountain kingdom, but the valley-folk want to take it. So they invade the mountain kingdom and kill the mountain people. They "turned the stone and looked beneath it… 'Peace on earth' was all it said." They have the treasure all along, but instead of wanting what they have, they search for happiness elsewhere. In their pursuit of the treasure, they destroy it. If they would just invest as much energy moving their own stones…

Poet Emily Dickinson tells the same story in a different way: "Eden is that old-fashioned house we dwell in every day without suspecting our abode until we drive away." All the stones we need to build our Stairway to Heaven are within reach. We just have to recognize them.

And we have to move them. "God doesn't make orange juice, God makes oranges," Jesse Jackson says. God doesn't make happiness either. He gives wonderful things to be happy about. We don't find ever-lasting love, despite what the songs say—we make love everlasting when we want the love we have.

Cherry blossoms swirling in the breeze across the streets of Washington, D.C. The haunting call of the loon on the early morning lake. The taste of pumpkin cheesecake. The aroma of lilacs floating in the spring air. (The aroma floats, not the lilacs.) The laughter of children. The warmth of a campfire on a chilly Algonquin autumn evening. When we really look at what we have, we see a beautiful world we should never take for granted. The Rolling Stones were wrong; we can get satisfaction.

∞ *Simply enough* ∞

I've outlived the millenium, though a year's worth of toilet tissue is stockpiled in our basement.
(If disaster hit, what would you really need?)

—*Columbus Dispatch* columnist Barbara Carmen

POP QUIZ:

Is the glass half empty or half full?
ANSWER: No, it's not. The glass is full. What happens when we don't take things for granted? We appreciate more, we accept that we have simply enough, we drink from a full glass. Your cup runneth over.

A multiple sclerosis patient wrote these words: "This disease is eating away at my body. There are days I can't see, can't hear, feel, taste or smell. But there are days when I can see and watch the sun dance on the leaves of our maple tree and shine golden in the hair of my children. On the days I can hear I awaken early and listen to the birds sing 'welcome' to the new day…. This is what makes life precious."

Stephen Hawking, the astronomer genius crippled by amyotrophic lateral sclerosis, advises, "When one's expectations are reduced to zero, one really appreciates everything one does." And one takes very few things for granted.

Ann Landers tells of four Amish people jailed for vandalizing a neighbor's farm. You might be aware that the austere Amish avoid modern conveniences, including electricity, zippers, cars, and telephones. After serving 72 days of their 90-day sentence, their jailer released them. His explanation? "The TV, the electric lights, telephone, and running water—I think they were starting to like it here." Welcome to the country club.

When we cease to take such commonplace conveniences as electricity and running water for granted, that's when we start to appreciate them. That's when we start to enjoy them. That's when we start to like it here.

A study of women at the University of Wisconsin shows that, after viewing images of harsher times and after describing imaginary personal tragedies, they rate their lives more satisfying than before the experiment. They recognize they have simply enough.

Let me help you feel satisfied by dispelling some harmful expectations. Few people in history enjoyed flush toilets (and the cleanliness they provide). Microwave ovens weren't even invented until a few years ago. Cars date back no more than a century. Toothpaste, light bulbs, stereos, frozen dinners, elevators, refrigerators (fresh meat in winter!), running water, telephones (never mind cell phones), washing machines, dishwashers, air conditioning: none of these existed for previous generations, and for most of the planet they still don't. Kind of makes automatic garage door openers seem almost ludicrous, doesn't it?

Of course, this sounds pretty preachy, like the father who tells his child, "In my day, I had to walk a million miles to school through ten feet of snow, and in the summer I had to do all the chores on the farm while it was so hot that my nose melted right off my face."

Exercise: . . . .
To really appreciate your luck, try to visualize what your
day would be like in some other time and place. Roll the
film in your mind's cinema. Picture yourself trudging to the
general store a couple miles away, rushing off to the out-
house in an emergency (in January in the Yukon), bathing
in cold water, dressing without zippers or spandex, and
scrubbing your clothes manually. I don't suggest forsaking
modern conveniences. Just visualize what life would be like
without them. Then open your eyes and look around you.
See how fortunate you are.

Is there a lesson here for parents? You bet! When we were young, our
parents told us there were starving kids in Africa, so we'd better eat
everything on our plates. Despite our most convincing pleas, they
refused to send those destitute kids our spinach and sardines and brus-
sels sprouts. I wanted to share some of my food with them (especially
the yucky stuff), but I didn't know their address. Could it be our parents
were less resolved to feed the world and more intent that we appreciate
our own bounty?

Poverty and destitution are foreign to the young mind. With so little
exposure to the world, most American kids know only video games, air
conditioning, and their personal chauffeurs (once upon a time called
"parents"). Lectures about starving kids in Africa (What's an Africa?)
don't sink in. A more effective way to instill appreciation is to take it all
away from them. Try these:

> **Camp** on your vacation. A breath of clean air refreshes a
> person's spirit. Leave behind the portable TV and the elec-
> tronic games, and avoid campgrounds with swimming
> pools. Let the kids appreciate the comforts of home.

If roughing it at a campground doesn't do the trick, step it up a notch. Volunteer their summer to a relief agency. There's no roughing it like the poorer regions of Ethiopia or India or Mali. As a bonus, they might learn the value of being a good citizen.

If the famine-ridden corners of the world fail to impress your offspring, if he's still unappreciative of his bounty, try the last, most desperate measure of all. Grab all the toys—the VCR, the TV, the videos, the CDs—and make a run for it. Wheeee! Hang on to them for a week, a month, whatever it takes.

In Chapter 2 we asked, "How much is enough?" Is "more" always the answer? Or do we already have enough, plus a box of chocolates and two trinkets to boot?

How do we know when we've "made it"? Well, here we are. Or should we want more and more things? Should we consume more and more resources like a fungus spreading across Starship Earth? At what point do we become happy? And is that before or after we chew our planet and spit it out?

When you want what you have, you move stones from the Great Wall of Misery to your Stairway to Heaven. Thank goodness.

CHAPTER 9

Happy Thanksgiving

Do not blame God for having created the tiger,
but thank him for not having given it wings.

—Indian proverb

Thanksgiving Day comes just once a year, but shouldn't we celebrate it every day? Thanksgiving allows us to feel and express our appreciation. And if we don't appreciate something, how can we be happy about it?

Psychologist Timothy Miller says that gratitude sometimes "causes resentment, envy, and disappointment to flee of their own accord." Los Angeles radio host Dennis Prager calls gratitude the "secret to happiness." I say, "Thank goodness for gratitude."

∞ *Feel grateful* ∞

What a wonderful life I've had!
I only wish I'd realized it sooner.

—French novelist Colette

Step one is to feel gratitude.

In the last chapter, we asked if the glass is half full or half empty, and we discovered the glass is full. Life is jam-packed with fantastic little things for which you can be grateful. Like the Girl Scouts who painted a mural over a graffiti-covered animal clinic in Dallas. Like spiders (thank you for eating the truly pesky bugs) and earthworms (thanks for tilling the soil). Little things include paper clips; at least I find *a few* things on my desk. Little things include plain vanilla ice cream, the perfect canvas on which to spread cantaloupe, blueberries, strawberries, banana. Yum. Little things we no longer take for granted.

Recognizing all we have to be grateful for is easy. Start with sight. If you are reading this book, consider how wonderful it is that you can see. Not everybody can. And many people who can see can't read. And many people who can read can't understand. And many people who can understand...I could go on, but if you understand what I mean, you have a lot to be thankful for.

Exercise:

Can you determine the value of all you have? Let's make a list. Start with your left eye. Would you sell it for—$10? $20? $100? $1,000? $1,000,000? Not at all? Now considering that your left eyeball has been sold, for how much would you sell your right eye? Keep doing this for every part of your body. I suspect you'll discover your true value is hundreds of times infinity. You are priceless.

Before reading any further, how about going through the same exercise with all the other things you have? Shelter, clothing, freedom of speech, freedom of movement, freedom of thought, fresh air, water, food, a library card, talent (can you dance, sing, sew, play pool, bowl, read, garden, tell jokes, bake a rich and great-tasting cheesecake, swim?)—everything you have. This will help you later in the chapter. You don't have to list every single pen or cracker or toothpick or shoe you own, but take about 15 minutes to jot down what comes to mind: freedoms, opportunities, friends, skills, knowledge, possessions—anything you have.

Now that you've completed the exercise, let's visit Dallas podiatrist Larry Lundy, who makes house calls—imagine that, house calls in the 21st century—to very, very appreciative patients. He says he, too, is grateful: "I see some things that make me feel so thankful, so grateful for what I have. I'm blessed."

Toronto Vice Principal Sandra Buie had this to say after being side-lined with meningitis: "In hospital, I saw people far worse off. At least I'd be getting out alive." There's nothing like an it-could-have-been-worse counterfactual to send gratitude forth. We'll read more about counterfactuals in a later chapter.

Gratitude is made from two words: *great* and *attitude*. If you have a great attitude, you have gratitude. Happiness is a choice. Decide whether you see the cloud or the silver lining. Decide whether your life is abuzz with joy or infested with mosquitoes. Decide whether the little things in your life are miracles or drudgery—whether they are stones in the Great Wall of Misery or in your Stairway to Heaven.

Commentator Andy Rooney is an expert at finding so much wrong with everyday, mundane situations. Your goal for happiness should be the reverse. Try to find whatever possible right in everyday, mundane situations. Those are the ingredients of chronic happiness.

Every day has a full 24 hours. That's a lifetime of joy and fulfillment for anyone who wants it. And every year has at least 365 days. That's just a few hours of joy for a dour spirit. Our days are numbered, so fill them with life. As Charles Darwin said, "A man who dares to waste one hour of life has not discovered the value of life."

Many of us don't take time to appreciate the wonders around us. The average time spent looking at any one exhibit at the National Zoo in Washington, D.C., is a zoomy five to 10 seconds. Is it better to "see" them all, or is it better to "experience" a few? There's no right answer, but it is worth thinking about.

POP QUIZ:
How long does a hippo stay submerged?
ANSWER: Ninety seconds on average. Most people think they stay under for much longer. As one tour guide explains, "Tourists just don't stay around long enough to watch them emerge."

The first step is to recognize your bounty.

The joy of thank you

Even though I clutch my blanket and growl when the alarm rings
each morning, thank-you, Lord, that I can hear.
There are many who are deaf.

— prayer

Step two is to express gratitude. We are all ventriloquists. When we give voice to an emotion, it comes to life. I know of no better example of a vocally grateful person than Chantal, my wife. When we clean the house together, she says, "Thank you for helping clean the house." As I write this, we just returned from a delicious, relaxing Thai brunch. On our way home, she said, "Thank you for coming with me to such a lovely brunch."

I want to emulate Chantal's excellent habit. At the same time, I feel some discomfort. Chantal's constant example pushes me beyond my comfort zone. I was not brought up saying *thank you*. I still have difficulty. In my head I know I want to, in my heart I know I should, but in my mouth it just doesn't always come forth. In the Introduction, I shared with you how I am still working to achieve maximum happiness. I explained that some habits take time to change. Well, this one is taking me some time.

Here's my opportunity to practice the habit of expressing my gratitude. Thank you for buying this book. Thank you for reading this book. And thank you for recommending this book to your friends (please?).

How can you learn to feel the joy of *thank you*? Just as there are endless ways to say, "I love you" (a dozen roses, breakfast in bed, a surprise dinner, a deep passionate kiss, a soothing massage, or just saying it), so, too, there are plenty of ways to say *thank you*.

An old Japanese gentleman couldn't understand that he needed coins, not a dollar bill, to pay the bus fare. After a helpful interloper came to his rescue, he performed a low, old-world bow. The Good Samaritan called this gesture "an elegant and unforgettable thank you."

Linh Duy Vo was saved from the Viet Cong by American soldiers. Now, living in the United States as a poet, he has dedicated much of his work to "every Vietnam vet (who) is my Daddy." What a beautiful way to say *thank you*.

In olden days, a man accompanying the Queen of England saw a hawk dive for the royal head. Lifting his bow, the man shot the hawk through the eye. In gratitude for his quick thinking and his true aim, the Queen named him Birdseye. The name was passed on through the generations to Clarence Birds Eye, the inventor of frozen food (and the founder of Birds Eye Frozen Foods). That's what I call gratitude that keeps on thanking.

Another way to express gratitude is simply to say, "Yay!" Does that sound a bit juvenile to you? Beneath your dignity? "Yay" is one of the most frequent words Chantal and I use around the house. Don't be shy to express your gratitude or your joy. You'll thank yourself for doing so.

See? There are so many ways to say thank you.

☜ *Bolsterism* ☞

*I feel that a coach is a teacher and I think that
a coach's greatest success is for the player to say
that this was the best class I had while I was in school.*

—Indiana University basketball coach Bob Knight

POP QUIZ:
Have you ever seen the geese flying overhead? The ones up front create updraft, making it easier for the others to fly. What's the role of the rear geese?
ANSWER: To honk, to encourage those up front to keep up their speed. To bolster the efforts of the lead geese.

You might have heard of boosterism. That's when the mayor of Oakland or Cleveland or Summutherland proclaims to anyone who'll listen what a great city it is—the best in the world! Boosterism is when the head of the Boston Red Sox or the Chicago White Sox brags about what a great team he has—the best in the world! It's when the President of General Motors or General Mills fires up the employees about what a great company they work for—the best in the world! That's boosterism.

Bolsterism is different. Instead of boosting, we bolster; we support and we strengthen. Bolsterism combines *waytogo* feedback with *wheretogo* directions. Toastmasters call this technique "evaluation," and it's the most useful skill I learned from Toastmasters.

A typical Toastmasters evaluation begins with a supportive, waytogo citation, such as:

> *Thank you for your speech. I really enjoyed it. You strode up in front of the lectern, took control, and spoke with confidence. Your speech was well organized, you spoke clearly, and made each point easy to understand. You made great eye contact with the audience, and I could see that you captivated the attention of everyone in the room.*

The evaluator then delivers fortifying wheretogo suggestions, such as:

> *Your topic was so upbeat, I would like to see you smile more. And it's such a lively topic, why not use your hands and arms? I would also like to see you use more floor space. I think you might have been holding back. For your next speech, let it loose. I'd like to see more of you in your speech.*

Most parents use bolsterism to train their children. It's the kind of gratitude your mother showed you when you did something right at a very young age. "Good job! You did that all by yourself. Mommy is so proud of you." Or, "You made this card especially for me? Thank you so much."

Bolsterism is one of the most powerful motivational tools a parent can use on a child, a teacher on a student, an employer on staff. If we don't say *thank you* to a spouse, a child, a co-worker, a client, a supplier, the boss…how will they know what we appreciate? How will they know what we want in the future? And how will we feel the gratitude?

Such positive feedback is the foundation of effective management. Yet how many managers do you know—maybe a former or current boss—who don't spend the time or effort to encourage, support, and commend employees for a job well done?

A Toastmasters club president explained how he applies some of what he learned at Toastmasters to his work environment. He told me how he started giving his employees positive feedback. "It doesn't take much. You just have to do it once or twice, and it's like you're paying them gold. They are so starved for recognition."

"But that's Management 101," I said.

"Yes," he replied. "But no one has ever done it there before. And everyone around started paying attention and whispering. Even my boss noticed and brought it up on my last performance evaluation. In fact, he even evaluated me in Toastmaster style, so I got both positive feedback and direction for improvement."

Why do supervisors so often overlook bolsterism? Perhaps because positive feedback and constructive criticism are all too often anything but positive or constructive. Toastmaster evaluations are so valuable to me that I now seek out feedback—and I keep pressing until I get some genuine suggestion for how to improve. Bolsterism helps others paint a positive portrait of themselves—a portrait that might just coax them out from behind the Mask of Success.

Washington, D.C., writer Judith Viorst illustrates the power of positive feedback with a story about her son, Tony, who proudly learned to tie his sneakers because Patrick Dowling tied his in front of the whole class. Judith assumed that Tony said to himself, "If Patrick Dowling can do it, I can do it."

"No," Tony replied. "I said, 'If they can clap for Patrick, they can clap for me.'"

Exercise:

I have a personal favor to ask of you. I want your feedback on this book. I want to know what you like and what you do not. Here are four questions for you to answer when you're done, if you would be so kind:

- What three things do you like most about this book?
- What could I do to make the next book even better?
- What comments would you offer about the writing style?
- What subjects in the book would you like me to explore in more detail in a future book?

With your help—your feedback—my next book will respond better to your personal needs. So please mark this page and send me your comments at dleonhardt@attglobal.net.

∞ *Just say it* ∞

I give great thank-you.

—unidentified woman,
explaining how she keeps her husband's endearment

For over a decade, I have worked as a consumer advocate. The popular image of a consumer advocate is that of an angry idealist who rants and raves about the injustices inflicted on common people by their governments and big corporations.

Sometimes that is true. Other times it is not. Many times I address public concerns about big business, in particular in the field of rising gasoline prices. And, yes, I see my share of government bungling, refusing to listen to the public, and spending too freely or hoarding too miserly.

My definition of a consumer advocate is a lobbyist with no expense account—but a lobbyist nonetheless. My job is to try to move habitat stones, which is not easy. As I often tell anyone who would listen, the most important words in lobbying are "thank you."

Why is *thank you* so important? Because if you want a politician or a bureaucrat to listen, you have to show appreciation for what they do for you. In most cases, the more appreciation you show, the better. When you think about it, this makes perfect sense. Would you keep helping someone who never says *thank you*? On the other hand, when someone expresses gratitude, don't you feel more inclined to help again? I use bolsterism to ensure government officials know both when we appreciate their actions and what we want them next to do.

Why don't we give thanks more often? Most people say thank you when they believe someone is doing them a favor...an unexpected bonus. Those same people often will not thank someone who is doing her job—something she is expected to do. You don't need to justify a *thank you*. Practice gratuitous gratitude. It is exactly because people expect their work to be taken for granted that they appreciate our thanks so much.

Your positive feedback brightens other people's day. And it will brighten your day, too.

Live in Graceland

*The car didn't kill me, the plane didn't crash
and the medical problems didn't stop me.
I've definitely had an angel on my shoulder.*

—Ohio bodybuilder Jill Thissen

Say grace. By "grace," I don't mean rote repetition of a prayer committed to memory. I mean vocally thank the Lord above for love, health, food, and anything else that went well today. Take the time before dinner to say grace.

Of course, God is not the only one to thank before dinner, which is great news for atheists. What about the farmer who grew the potatoes on your plate? Say "Thanks" to him. What about Mother Nature? Or Father Time? What about those who suffered for your freedom?

How about thanking Gideon Sundback. He invented the zipper in 1913. Imagine what life would be like without zippers! Thank you, Gideon. What about all the others who invented things you use today? What about your ancestors, responsible for your very life? Whether you believe in God or not, there is value in once a day vocalizing gratitude for your blessings. That's one way to appreciate them, one way to make yourself happier for them.

Exercise: ....

Set up a system to say grace as a family at the dinner table, before bed, or over breakfast. If you live alone, try approaching a neighbor. Or try saying grace with colleagues to start or end the workday. Stopping in a church along the way home works for some people.

Another option to "vocalize" your appreciation is through a gratitude journal.

There are numerous ways to prepare a gratitude journal. Remember the song from *The Sound of Music*? "Cream-colored ponies and crisp apple strudels. Doorbells and sleigh bells and schnitzel with noodles. Wild geese that fly with the moon on their wings." These are a few of Maria von Trapp's favorite things. And when she simply remembers her favorite things she doesn't feel so bad.

Several people maintain gratitude Web sites. Others write their gratitude lists on shared Web sites. Of course, there is the traditional way of writing down everything positive that happens today in the form of a diary. You could even name it *Thursday's greatest hits*. Or *Thanks for the Memories.*

It doesn't matter how you express your gratitude, only that you do. In expressing it, you feel it. In feeling it, you make yourself happier.

So take time to smell the roses...but even more importantly, to appreciate them. Oh yes, and thank you for reading this chapter.

HABIT # 4

Learn, then burn

Yesterday is ashes; tomorrow wood.
Only today does the fire burn brightly.

—Eskimo proverb

What's done is done. But sometimes we cling to the past anyway. And that can be a wonderful thing. Our minds' cinemas teem with beautiful memories. Maybe a certain odor carries you back to your classroom or to the playground. Maybe there's a song that reminds you of your first date. Maybe you reminisce over old photos.

Or maybe you cling to pain from the ghosts of anger past.

Our memory vault overflows with images, some sweet, some sour. Some accurate, some less so. We hold on tighter to some memories than to others. Habit #4 is all about picking and choosing. Don't give up those wonderful memories that fill you with joy. Those are precious. Those are blessings for us to count.

The sour memories, those that carry pain, have no place in our lives. So you had a bad experience; maybe you suffered pain, embarrassment, anger, guilt. Find out what you need to learn—what lesson the experience can teach you—learn it, then burn your bridge to pain.

Before we go any further, this habit deserves a great big caveat. Some painful memories linger in unpredictable ways and color other things we do. Some ghosts simply won't ignite on a whim. That's why psychotherapists exist. If your match won't set the memories afire, please speak with a professional therapist. (Don't be shy. Self-improvement is something to be proud of.) This book is about habits, and the following three chapters are about letting go of pain on a day-to-day basis. And that's all many people need. But a book—any book—is unlikely to help resolve complex, deep-rooted psychological issues.

We're here to raise your daily happiness. So let's learn from our pain, then burn the memories.

Chapter 10

Who you gonna blame?

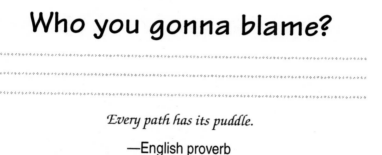

Every path has its puddle.

—English proverb

Men who nick themselves while shaving blame the blade. Women nickers blame themselves. So who's really to blame? Nobody. Blame is the most useless reaction to any event, big or small.

Blame is like a lightening bolt. It strikes in stormy weather. It fixes on a specific target. It causes horrible damage.

Lightening is like blame in another way. We think of lightening as a one-way bolt from heaven to earth. But lightening often strikes from tall objects upwards. In truth, it's hard to be sure which way lightening heads at 100,000 miles per second. It's often hard to tell in which direction blame should be assigned. How often do two people blame each other for something? Blame is useless. Does it matter which way the lightening heads when it destroys our home? Does it matter who's to blame, the clouds or the house?

POP QUIZ:

What's the difference between finger pointing and finger painting?

ANSWER: Finger painting is more colorful. Other than that, they're both childish games.

Uproot blame. Expel the word from your vocabulary.

 ## *River rage*

> *I learned a long time ago that if you're going to throw
> a club in anger, throw it in front of you
> so you won't have to go back and pick it up.*

—President Ronald Reagan

In the dry season, Zambia's Luangwa River shrivels up, until little is left but a dotted line of puddles in a swamp of mud. Most animals leave for moister ground. Not the hippos. They just squeeze into a shrinking pool of water. The more crowded they become, the nastier they act. They bear their teeth at one another. They pick fights. It's river rage.

We read daily about road rage, air rage, parking lot rage, supermarket eight-items-or-less checkout line rage. Stressed out and impatient, it's so easy to blow up at one another. And it's so easy to feel righteous about it. But it's hard to feel happy about it.

Anger is the junk food of emotions. You might have heard that ambitious and aggressive Type A people are prone to stress and heart attacks. This doesn't sound healthy. But Duke University researchers report that not all Type A people flirt with heart attacks and stress breakdowns— just those with high hostility levels. Hostility leads to calcium deposits in the heart, which increases the risk of heart attacks and other afflictions. Mouth-to-mouth recrimination is no better for our bodies than for our spirits.

According to Pierre Thiffault, of the University of Montreal Driving Simulation Lab, aggression distracts from other goals: "Aggression takes energy. You are *busy* being aggressive, and that draws away from the driving task."

Driving along a winding Pennsylvania road, a man approaches a long curve. A car approaches from the opposite direction. As it passes, a woman sticks out her head and yells, "Pig!" Shocked, the man yells back after her, "You're not so great yourself." As he turns his attention back to the road, he crashes into a large pig. A hasty assumption, a red-hot temper, a crash course in jumping to conclusions.

I had a similar experience in a remote campground. Halfway through the week, a stampede of characters drove away the tranquility as they crammed into the two nearby sites. They brought half a dozen vehicles and at least as many kids. Above the newly elevated noise level, I suddenly heard the most terrifying wail. Then I heard it again. And once more. At first, I had no clue what it was, until I noticed one man…tuning his bagpipe. He spent half an hour tuning. I was livid.

As the sun approached the horizon, he went down to the strip of beach behind our sites and started playing a variety of tunes. My temper mellowed, and curiosity drew my lawn chair and me down to the sand, too. When the bottom of the sun tickled the top of the distant hills, the Scotsman waded into "Amazing Grace" and continued until the sun melted out of site. It was a truly inspirational moment. When one of the ladies from their group approached me later that evening to apologize for the noise, I told her the noise didn't bother me. In a moment of irritation, remember that a closed mouth gathers no feet.

Paul took his prescription to the pharmacist, who handed him a small plastic jar with a dozen little pills. Paul squinted to see the tiny pills, but his eyes opened wide when he saw the $212 price. "What?! All that money just for such tiny pills?"

The pharmacist picked up the jar and stared at the pills. "Well, I suppose if you'd prefer, I could pull the medication in really, really, really BIG pills," he offered. Paul decided to calm down. All things considered, anger doesn't consider all things.

Iowa legislators felt compelled to introduce a bill to protect minor league umpires and referees from attacks by players, coaches, spectators, and parents. I had barely finished tsk-tsking in disbelief, when I read about a football brawl (would that be a footbrawl?) in Florida among more than 100 players, coaches, spectators, and parents. Who says it's just a game?

∞ *Temper lost and found* ∞

I hear you have an excellent dairy industry here.

—Canadian politician Stockwell Day,
after protesters doused him in chocolate milk

POP QUIZ:
Does it help to vent your anger?
ANSWER: No. You might have heard it's better to vent your anger than to hold it inside. Not true. Like a wildfire on the open prairie, venting anger can send it blazing out of control. Anger breeds anger. You've heard that the more love you give, the more love you have. Well, it's equally true that the more we lose our temper, the more we find it. Psychologists tell us that venting anger or talking out your feelings rehearses the emotion rather than dispelling it. Losing your temper is an oxymoron.

Sure, holding it in or "steaming" is harmful. In fact, research shows that repressed anger promotes cancer. But it turns out that it is not so much the repression as it is the lack of intimacy and connectedness, which causes repression, that promotes cancer. Suppression of anger is a symptom of feeling alone, of not being able to share how we feel. But full steam ahead will only get you, well, more steam.

Narkey Terry and Billy Canipe lost their cool on the George Washington Parkway in Virginia. Theirs is typical of the road rage stories we hear about these days. At 80 miles an hour, they took their duel across the median and hit two other cars. The result was three deaths and one prison sentence. They lost more than just their cool.

Here are just a few examples of how anger can get you into trouble:
• In France, an angry baker smears jam on a car parked in his delivery zone. He is fined $100.
• A San Antonio ice cream truck driver finds out that playing "Pop! Goes the Weasel" repeatedly over the loudspeaker can be a one-way ticket to the emergency room.
• Two Westport, Connecticut, shoppers trade blows over who should be first at a checkout line.

• A British Columbia man strangles his girlfriend in a dispute over how to interpret a biblical passage.
• In Pennsylvania, a man shoots his friend through the heart with a bow and arrow during a Monopoly® game because he "wanted to be the car rather than the thimble or the hat."
• German beer garden patrons club a businessman to death because his cell phone is "really loud," has "one of those terrible melodies," and he refused to turn it off.

What long shadows little things cast on our hearts.

On a larger scale, El Salvador won a World Cup soccer match by a score of 3-2 over neighboring Honduras…on a penalty kick. Wild riots ignited both capital cities, and seven days later war was declared. Two thousand soldiers lost their lives, the Central American Common Market disbanded, and both nations suffered a shortage of food. Oh, yeah…the El Salvador team was eliminated in the next round.

How can you climb your Stairway to Heaven if you're too busy gnarling at people to one side or the other? Anger is a natural emotion. It prepares us to defend our kill. To flee. To fight. To survive in the wild. But we don't roam the jungle any more, and anger no longer serves a useful purpose.

Is it a sign of weakness to back down or to look like a pushover? The Dalai Lama says this: "Since patience and tolerance come from an ability to remain firm and steadfast and not be overwhelmed…one should not see tolerance or patience as a sign of weakness, or giving in, but rather as a sign of strength, coming from a deep ability to remain firm." If you've ever heard the expression "strong enough to bend," you know what the Dalai Lama means.

I remember as a child driving Chicago's Lakeshore Boulevard (Okay, I wasn't driving at the time). It would bend for inbound commuters, as the median moved over to accommodate the increased flow of traffic. And every afternoon it bent again for outbound commuters as the median sidled back to where it had been. Flexible, accommodating, strong.

Exercise:

Think of all the situations that make you angry—all the situations in which you either vent your anger or let it stew inside. Understanding where, when, and how you become angry is the first step to losing...er, finding...er, stopping your temper.

∞ *Ready. Blame. Fire.* ∞

He says, "I drink because she nags."
She says, "I nag because he drinks."

—psychotherapist Michael Greene

BLAM!!! Blame even sounds like firing a gun. Or like smashing into the Great Wall of Misery at full speed. Pin-the-blame-on-the-donkey is a dangerous game to play. The very concept of blame is adversarial. It assumes someone must be "at fault." It pits you against me. It assumes there is an "us" and a "them."

You might guess that Sarah Sheep is tempted to blame Bray Goat for falling into the well: "Just like a silly old goat to get us into this mess! I don't know why I hang around with you." And Bray Goat is not immune from mouth-to-mouth recrimination either: "Clumsy sheep. If you hadn't tripped, we wouldn't be fending off stones in a dump of a well." Fortunately, they both came to their senses, realizing they are in this together. Only by cooperating will they climb out of the well.

Blame is easy to assign, especially when you haven't been in the other person's shoes. It's even easier to express over the Internet, where we can vent frustration without ever looking into the eyes of the person we hurt. We live in a click-and-vent society, where it seems easier to throw our multiple-choice stones at someone else than to move them from the Wall to our Stairway. (Maybe that's why we call it a cursor.)

There are plenty of good reasons to blame and to vent. He cut in line. She stole my parking space. His cat was in my garden. Aren't those great reasons to blame? There are gazillions of reasons to blame…if that's what you're looking for. But was he trying to delay you, or was he just in a hurry? Was she trying to keep you from parking, or was she just after the best spot? Was the cat trying to ruin your work, or was he just being a cat?

Of course, you have the right to be upset, just as you have the right to stick your tongue in the toaster or staple your ear to the door post. (Don't try this at home, folks. Only a professionally certified idiot can perform these stunts without causing inconvenient brain damage.)

Every now and then a pedestrian crosses the street on a green light, even though a car is bearing down on him against a red. Of course, he has the *right* to cross the street. He has the "right" of way. But whether he hits the car or the car hits him…who gets hurt? Does it really matter that he was dead right? So the question is: "Do you prefer to be right (**OUCH!**) or happy?"

The court of law, in its noble pursuit of justice, often seems to be more like a circus of blame. Celine Dion sues the *National Enquirer* for reporting she's pregnant with twins. Carol Burnett sues for implying she was drunk in public. Clint Eastwood sues for publishing a fake interview with him. One Ohio lady claims $25,000 in damages from a neighbor for permanent physical harm from…negligently squirting her with a garden hose. A cancer patient sues his doctor for living longer than the doctor predicted. Is it just me, or is this nuts?

Earlier in the book I raised the silly specter of governments suing tobacco companies for following the government's own laws. Sure, the tobacco companies might be black-hearted scoundrels, and their products might have blackened more than a few lungs, but isn't it the government's responsibility to stop such catastrophes from happening? But it's so much easier to blame.

POP QUIZ:
What's the relationship between blame and control?
* Synonyms
* Homonyms
* Antonyms
* Cause and effect
* Predator and prey

ANSWER: Antonyms. Although if you answered predator and prey, you're not far off.

Pin-the-blame-on-the-donkey is a game we play blindfolded. When we blame someone else for our misfortunes, we cede control to that person. We give up. If we blame ourselves, and focus on the blame, we simply feel miserable without improving anything. If you want control, take responsibility and correct what went wrong. Don't blame someone, not even yourself.

∞ *The guilt quilt* ∞

Guilt is a gift that keeps on giving.

—humorist Erma Bombeck

Two old women in the same New England town died at the same time. The son of the first blamed himself, "If only I had sent my mother to Florida and gotten her out of this cold and snow, she would be alive today." The son of the other woman said, "If only I hadn't insisted on my mother's going to Florida, she would be alive today. That long airplane ride, the abrupt change of climate, was more than she could take. It's my fault she's dead."

Anger comes easily, blame comes easily, and so does guilt, which is really self-blame. It's amazing how comforting a blanket of guilt can feel—like a warm guilt quilt.

Parents lay guilt on their children to control them, to lead them in the right direction. The same parents later lay guilt on themselves for every failing of their grown-up children, as if they ever really had total control and complete responsibility for their children's lives.

It's important to take responsibility for our actions. It's important to be able to say, "Oops. I goofed." It's important to recognize mistakes. Otherwise, how can we correct them? How can we learn?

But it's useless to wrap ourselves up in the guilt quilt. Like spotmisserism, guilt draws attention away from our accomplishments, our value, our blessings. It serves no purpose to say, "Aargh! I'm such an idiot!" If we're mired in guilt, how can we find ways to correct our mistakes? Guilt is, in fact, a sneaky way to deny responsibility. Being an "idiot" is a great excuse for avoiding response ability and for not correcting errors.

∞ *Caught in the act* ∞

You're only human.
You're supposed to make mistakes.

—singer Billy Joel in "Only Human"

Embarrassment cuts into our happiness, just as anger, blame, and guilt do. President Franklin Roosevelt, in his years of declining health, asked to keep his wheelchair out of sight. Respect for the presidency compelled the media to comply. That would never happen in Mediadom today, but times change.

What doesn't change is human pretense. Of course, there's nothing wrong with preferring a certain look or cultivating a certain image, as long as the image is genuine and as long as we do it for ourselves, not for others.

The image we cultivate must be real, otherwise we deny who we are. As we already saw in Chapters 6 and 7, when we feel ashamed of who we are, when we try to be someone we are not, when we fail to value our own uniqueness, happiness escapes us.

Likewise, the image we cultivate has to be for ourselves—because that's how we want to be, not because we think that's how others want us to be.

Few people portray a totally honest image to others. We all wear masks. As with lots of things in life, it's a matter of balance. The question we need to ask ourselves is whether the image we cultivate is who we really are.

Hugh was waiting in line at the bank. When he figured nobody was looking, he decided to pick his nose. (Sorry about the imagery.) Just as he was removing his finger, he caught the eye of his boss's wife. Embarrassed, he spent the next seven years avoiding her. Embarrassment haunts us a bit like guilt—even if we know we didn't really do anything wrong.

✺ *Explain this!* ✺

You can go all out and squeeze joy, happiness
and fulfillment out of life, or you can atrophy.
It is all in the way you decide to view your situation.

—nurse to newly-disabled Jim Porter

Not everything we react to negatively makes us angry or guilty, nor do we always blame someone. Sometimes we blame some*thing.* Sometimes we simply feel irritated, upset, impatient. I get that way with my computer, with photocopy machines—come to think of it, with any machine that fails to understand the importance of doing exactly what I want it to do.

Have you ever felt that whichever checkout line you choose, yours will be the slowest? Or whenever you want an elevator to go up, the first one to arrive is heading down? The world really isn't out to get us; it just seems that way sometimes. For instance, if you're waiting for an elevator near the bottom of a building, you probably want to go up. But most of the elevators are probably above you, so the next one to arrive is most likely to be heading down. See? The world's not out to get you.

Studies show that people rarely act in an objective manner. We interpret information emotionally and act on our interpretations. For optimists, this works wonderfully. Optimists blame less and feel happy more. It works in reverse for pessimists. They blame more and are less likely to feel good about themselves or their situation.

Optimists are also more likely to remain healthy. Once sick, pessimists tend to recuperate more slowly. Pessimism, passivity, and hopelessness also make death more likely. One seminal study links stable, global, and internal explanatory styles as key health risks.

A stable explanatory style would be: "It's never going to change, I'm stuck with this forever, if not longer." It's when our mind's cinema replays scenes of failure, disappointment, guilt.

A global explanatory style is all encompassing: "Now look, it's ruined my entire day." Or, "This affects everything I do."

An internal style is self-depreciating and might inspire guilt: "It's all my fault." Or, "I can't do anything right." Rodney Dangerfield expresses this style with his "I can't get no respect" line.

Exercise:
Take a moment to think about how you react to events: things that happen to you, things you do, things you do with others, etc. Try to identify if you use any of the three explanatory styles listed above.

In this chapter, we look at how we might react negatively to events, both big and small. In the next chapter, we'll look at how we can deal with those reactions. One of the tools we use is our explanatory style.

CHAPTER 11

Take your hand off the hot stove

To kick with sore toe only hurts foot.

—Japanese proverb

Elsie is a food production manager. She works hard. She focuses her energy. She brings out the best in her staff, and they love her for it. Her department is the most productive in the company.

Everyone thought Elsie would become the new vice president. But Sam plays politics better than Elsie. When Elsie heard about Vice President Sam, she was furious. She complained to her colleague, Mike, "It's not fair. I work hard and get results...better results than Sam. That was *my* promotion. Sam is just a sneaky, rotten, no good son-of-a-*****!"

Over the next two months, Mike saw Elsie avoid Sam. He heard her make snide comments about him. He saw her brood. Where was the Elsie everyone loved so much?

So Mike approached Elsie. "You're still very upset about Sam," Mike ventured.

Elsie shot back, "Sam stole my job. I have every right to be angry."

"But you're clearly in pain. Why hold your hand on a hot stove?" Mike asked.

"I'm not holding my hand on a hot stove," Elsie replied. "Sam is."

"Sam sure burned you," Mike agreed. "But Sam walked away, and you're still holding your hand on the stove. Why not take it off so you can enjoy life again?"

Dr. David's diagnosis: stove-hold burns, third degree. There's a lesson in there somewhere.

∞ *Holding grudges* ∞

Nobody ever forgets where he buried a hatchet.

—humorist Kin Hubbard

Rudolf and Adolph (Adi) Dassler founded Adidas® shoes. After a falling out, Rudolf left to found Puma shoes, and the two survived in a state of uncivil war. When Adolph died, the two brothers had not spoken for 29 years. John and William Kellogg founded—you guessed it—Kellogg's® cereals. In a spat over whether the cereals should be healthy or marketable, the two brothers traded their brotherly love for a life of mutual litigation. When John died, the brothers hadn't spoken in 33 years. Can you believe that?

The Reverend Barbara King observes, "The injustice itself continues to live in the person's mind as though it happened five minutes ago… The painful experience continues to live in today's reality." Stove-hold burn is self-inflicted pain—and totally meaningless suffering.

LINDA COULD NOT CONVINCE THE STOVE TO STOP BURNING HER

One leader of the Warsaw uprising cried out years later, "If you could lick my heart, it would poison you." Unfortunately, no Nazi will lick his heart, so the poison remains there in his heart, inflicting damage on him instead. Even when the sin is great, holding a grudge hurts the victim more than the perpetrator.

You can't go back in time to move foundation stones. Unfortunately, some people try. And even if others point this out, someone heading the wrong way is rarely inclined to listen to advice.

Marriage counsellors report that one of the most destructive ways to crush a marriage is to revive past arguments in current fights. There's no point burying the hatchet if you leave the handle sticking out. Leave that to the Hatfields and McCoys.

And leave it to kids to teach us adults a lesson on grudges. Judy and Charles brought their children over to Loraine and Mack's house. While the adults played euchre, the kids flitted from one game to another…until a fight broke out. The parents somehow broke up the fight. Ten minutes later, as the kids were deep into some other game, the adults were still dueling over whose kid was at fault.

Grade 2 teacher Phyllis Walker marvels at how children can be at each other's throats one minute and best pals the next. "Why is it that grown-ups are so miserable?" she muses. "They hold on to so much this and that about other people." And holding on to thises and thats isn't good for your heart or your blood pressure. One study reveals that releasing all those thises and thats makes a person three times more likely to survive a heart attack.

POP QUIZ:

When they are hot, what do you call those round things on the stove? You might call them "elements" or "burners" or simply "**OUCH!!!**" But what's their proper name?

ANSWER: Grudges. Just call them grudges. There really is no point holding on to a grudge. We hurt nobody but ourselves when we hold on to a grudge.

Holding a grudge is the first step to revenge. In fact, revenge is a violent outcome of holding a grudge. Somehow we feel the other person should be hurt because we are. Oops. Maybe we forgot the lesson our parents taught us that two wrongs don't make a right and that two pains do not feel better than one. And since we're practicing our math, doubling our fists won't give us four hands.

When it comes to revenge, the old adage, "Be careful what you wish for—it might come true" is especially valid. A middle-aged woman discovered that her husband had been cheating on her. A little further digging revealed that he had a voracious appetite for just about anybody with a set of mammary glands. Infuriated, the woman filed for divorce, hired a high-priced lawyer, and proceeded to take her former husband to the proverbial cleaners.

Of course, these things are never easy, and, in the end, the only people to get rich are the divorce lawyers. With every day, the woman grew angrier. She wanted revenge. "I wish I could get him," she whispered one night. **POOF!** A genie appeared.

"I am the Divorce Genie," he announced. "I can grant you three wishes."

The woman thought about it a while, then as a wicked smile spread across her face, she replied, "First, I want him to lose all his girlfriends."

"It is done," the Genie spoke. They heard harsh words, a slap or two, and watched three half-naked young ladies hurry from his house.

"Second, I want him to contract AIDS," she continued.

"So be it," the genie asserted. They heard a cry of agony coming from the house.

"Third, I want all his money," the woman finished.

"Your wish is my command," replied the genie. **POOF**! The genie was gone. To her horror, the woman found herself in bed beside her husband, who was wearing nothing but an ear-to-ear grin.

"You know," he softly spoke. "I might soon die of AIDS, but I'll enjoy every bit of the trip."

A moment of revenge can also destroy what took years to build, whether that's a relationship, a fellow human being, a work of art, or much more. Consider what can happen in the wink of an eye:

• Rome was burned to the ground in a matter of days.
• The guillotine removed King Louis XVI's head in a flash.
• In only a few hours, a stubborn iceberg sank the *Titanic*.
• It took just an instant to kill President Kennedy.
• The happy life of Pompeii was destroyed with a single angry breath from Mount Vesuvius.

When colonial Ceylon became independent Sri Lanka, revenge and counter-revenge led to the civil war between the Tamils and the Sinhalese. Similar story, different characters, and welcome to Northern Ireland. Zoom across Europe to Palestine, and we see the same story being replayed once more. Was it not revenge for its humiliating defeat in World War I that led so many Germans to embrace the Nazi doctrine?

Let's be careful what we do and how we feel. Don't believe a word of it when they say revenge is sweet. It's not. Revenge implies that your happiness is a product of how someone else feels—and we know that's a lie. Forgiveness is sweet, because you can control that.

John Corbett, one of North America's best market researchers, called me up one day: "The client stiffed me. They just walked out on me. But they are my favorite coffee brewer, so at least I had a fine cup of coffee." Stonemason John moved his stones instead of holding a grudge. Lesson learned.

∞ *Marinating in Why me? sauce* ∞

I feel like the boy who stubbed his toe;
I am too big to cry and too badly hurt to laugh.

—Abraham Lincoln after losing a Senate election

When Joan Abery died, she had lived for 35 years sheltered only by twigs and umbrellas. She had refused to set foot in her home after being jilted at the altar.

Cartoonist Charles Schulz was about to propose to red-haired Donna Johnson just when she chose someone else. In memory of his own unrequited love, Charlie Brown's unrequited love went to the Little Red-Haired Girl.

Brooding, like holding a grudge, is no way to build your Stairway to Heaven. Why marinate yourself in a sauce of pain?

Here's a helpful game you can play. One day, Chantal was having a really rough time and suddenly felt as if she was drowning. "What a horrible day this is," she moaned. So I tried something I had heard about. I drew four columns on a sheet of paper and divided each into six rows, forming 24 boxes. Each box was an hour in the day. I asked, "How was your first hour, from midnight to 1:00 a.m.?"

She stared at me (as if I was out of my mind, no doubt!), "I was asleep."

"Fine, and how was your sleep? Restful? Fretful? Did you sleep well?"

"I slept well," she responded.

"Great. That means the first hour of your day was excellent. What about the second?"

We continued this game all the way to 4:00 p.m., when we hit a snag. All sorts of things seemed to happen at once. That was not a happy hour. So I tallied up the day: 16 good hours and one bad hour. "So, how was your day," I asked.

Chantal grinned, "It was great." Now that she knew the day wasn't completely shot, she was able to focus on fixing the things that had been going wrong in the last hour. Since then, we've both used this game when one of us feels overwhelmed. We found a way to avoid the global explanatory style of, "Now look, it's ruined my entire day." Another lesson learned.

Golfer Tom Watson was eight under par and set to win the $300,000 Byron Nelson Classic. Then weather and luck combined forces to send him four over par. (For those who don't play golf, that's not good.) A reporter asked him about how he felt. "It doesn't upset me. Golf is not a fair game," he responded. He moved his stones.

Most people tend to ask the question, "Why me?" if they run into a stroke of bad luck or if things go wrong. The only logical answer is, "Why not me?" Without that answer, we might be tempted to assume everything is our fault. "If only I had…" or "If only I hadn t…" or "I am so clumsy/foolish/mean/pick-your-self-demeaning-adjective." But the simple truth is: "Why not me?"

When someone asks, "What's eating you?" they really mean it. Brooding eats away at the best part of you: your happiness. Brooding is quite simply good for neither the spirit nor the flesh. Eight years after 122 people had their first heart attack, 21 of the 25 most pessimistic were dead. Just six of the most optimistic died. Optimistic people don't brood; they look forward. They avoid that stable explanatory style that says, "Hey, things suck now, so they probably always will." The optimist avoids painting herself into a corner facing the wall with nothing but a hot stove to hold onto. Toss that *Why me?* sauce in the trash.

What's eating you?

x Anger?
x Jealousy?
x Fear?
x Embarrassment?
x Guilt?
x Envy?
x Regret?

∽ *Out, damned spot!* ∽

Rolling in the muck is not the best way of getting clean.

—author Aldous Huxley

POP QUIZ:

Lady MacBeth spent her latter days screaming, "Out, damned spot!" What did she mean by this?

- Her dog kept piddling on the carpet.
- She kept spilling ketchup on her white blouse.
- She was filming a cleanser commercial.
- She was cursing her all-consuming guilt.

ANSWER: That's right, she welded herself to her guilt and cursed all the way to the grave. That's no way to spend a life. Let go.

So you made a bad decision. You had to pay the piper. You can't return and demand your money back. You can't erase decisions you made. So let's not think about what went wrong. Let's focus on the best path to follow from this point forward.

Philip and Jane Dick were born premature, but after six weeks, Jane died. For the rest of his life, Philip wrote to Jane in his journals to ease his guilt for hogging their mother's milk. He used the internal explanatory style: "It's all my fault."

When good luck strikes, you might also ask, "Why me? I don't deserve to be so lucky." Guilt sometimes emerges from winning the same award over and over, or from someone going out of his way to help you. We appreciate winning and receiving help, but if we get a lot of it, we might feel guilty. "Why me?" we ask. And the logical answer is, of course, "Why not me?"

It's one thing to feel guilt when you do something wrong. It's another thing to hold on to the guilt, especially when you've done nothing wrong. Guilt can totally consume a person, but it won't help someone we've wronged. Out, damned guilt!

⌇ *Running in circles* ⌇

"The horror of that moment," the King went on, "I shall never forget."
"You will, though," the Queen said,
"if you don't make a memorandum of it."

—author Lewis Carroll

The problem with brooding, holding grudges, and guilt is that they just keep taking us back where we were. It's not just that we relive our misery. It's also that we never get the chance to move forward. They send us on a Groundhog Day trip. Remember Bill Murray in the movie *Groundhog Day*? Each day was the same day. Each morning, he awoke to the same song on the radio. He had to relive the same day over and over and over until he learned the lesson of the day.

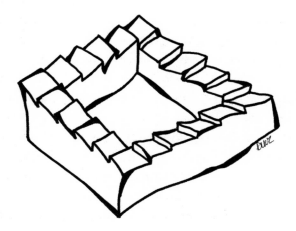

Like a dog chasing its tail, we run in circles when we brood. It's sort of like climbing that famous trick staircase. We keep climbing, but we never seem to get anywhere. We always wind up back where we started. That staircase will never get us to heaven.

We want to climb our Stairways to Heaven. We don't want to start each day back where we were. We must put the past behind us so we can focus on what matters ahead. Cartoonist Lynn Johnston, of *For Better or For Worse*® fame, recalls how she was abused as a child ...and how she felt she had later mistreated her own son. It's a well many abused children fall into as adults. But Lynn Johnston climbed out of the well. She saw where she was heading and sought professional help.

Shake off the stones, step up. Shake off the stones, step up. Shake off the stones, step up. Sarah Sheep feels like she's reliving the same steps over and over (and she is). But she has to keep focused ahead so that she can do what it takes to get past the stones falling on her back.

Think of it this way: if you do the same thing the same way, you get the same results. If you keep buying goldfish, and you keep feeding them pepper, and they keep dying, stop feeding them pepper. Okay, I'm stretching it, but do you see my point? If anger doesn't make you happy, if brooding doesn't carry joy, if guilt doesn't inspire satisfaction, try a new approach. Stop replaying the pain.

One way to escape the trick staircase is to read your life as a book—even this book. You finish a chapter, then you start a new one. You carry the lessons from the previous chapter and apply what you learned. But you focus on the chapter you are reading now (which in this case is Chapter 11).

Or think of life as a winding switchback road, like the ones that trace the mountains overlooking Palm Springs or carve their way through the St. Gotthard Pass in Switzerland. As the road curves, we catch glimpses of where we've been and what we left behind. But we continue to ascend, we continue to advance, we continue moving forward.

❀ *David's Incredible Time Machine* ❀

I don't mind getting old because the alternative is dying young.

—singer Kenny Rogers

There might be no magic wand or secret to happiness, but there is David's Incredible Time Machine to help you give the cold shoulder to all those trivial, pesky annoyances of daily life. You know the ones. The rabid driver who tries to run you down. The inconsiderate doofus who deposits gum in the automatic teller. The movie theatre snorasaurus. The computer that keeps failing the crash test. (Or am I the only dummy to suffer that indignity?) Let's immunize ourselves to those pesky, trivial annoyances that overshadow all the wonderful little things we have.

David's Incredible Time Machine is truly a miracle. It requires no software, no hardware, no storage space, and, as a special bonus, it sports your choice of colors and flavors. The operating instructions are as follows:

Step 1: Wait for something irritating.

Step 2: Fast-forward your mind 10 years.

Step 3: Linger a moment to savor the happiness you've enjoyed for 10 years, thanks to the nine habits of maximum happiness you put into practice.

Step 4: Ask yourself this question: "Will this trivial, pesky annoyance matter now (10 years later)?"

Step 5: Answer, "No."

Step 6: Rewind to the present, fully immune to those pesky, trivial annoyances (and free to enjoy yourself).

Step 7: Repeat when necessary.

David's Incredible Time Machine is an exclusive offer only for readers of *Climb Your Stairway to Heaven.*

Exercise:
Put David's Incredible Time Machine to work for you.

CHAPTER 12

Don't look back

To take revenge is often to sacrifice oneself.

—African proverb

Yogi Berra said, "When you get to a fork in the road, take it." People might snicker at this, but they should pay attention. No matter where you are, you face a fork in the road. You can choose any of the paths ahead. Behind you lies the handle of the fork. Alas, you cannot choose to go back.

POP QUIZ:
Why did Swedish chemist Alfred Nobel establish the Nobel Prize?
ANSWER: He established the prize in his will to atone for inventing dynamite. Although we can't undo our mistakes, or those of others, we can sometimes compensate for them. Like Alfred Nobel, we can do this only by looking forward. Happiness can't be found staring into the rear view mirror.

ꕥ *Painful memories* ꕥ

To this day, I'm glad I didn't let my anger get the upper hand.

—Hartford teacher Roger Calip

Pain is not all bad. The ravages of leprosy are due not to the disease rotting the flesh, but rather to the absence of pain. Without pain to warn lepers of torn tissue, they literally rub their skin off running and scraping and banging even when bones are showing. We need pain to say, "Whoa. Stop *doing* that!"

The key is to learn the lessons pain tries to teach us. Then let go of the stove.

If our mind's cinema keeps replaying everything that went wrong in the past, how can we ever be happy? The longer we live, the more things will have gone wrong…the more things we replay…the more unhappy we become. And that means chronic misery.

Hindsight is 20/20 vision. It's easy to see the past, but much harder to envisage the future. It's cleanup time. Empty the drawers and get rid of the old film footage so we can focus our vision on the path before us.

Think about the home videos people watch. They replay the videos of their weddings, not their divorces. Why replay painful memories in the cinema of your mind? Reruns of joy—repeat. Reruns of pain—delete.

In the Cinderella tale, the carriage turns into a pumpkin at midnight. Everything that happens to it during the day vanishes, and it's ready to start the new day as a fresh, new, and delicious pumpkin. Mmmm-mmm. Can you follow that example? Can you clear your mind, your heart, your soul of anything negative at the end of the day? The Bible says, "…let not the sun go down upon your wrath…" (Ephesians 4:26). Chantal wisely makes that a habit of her relationship with me. At midnight, all anger, all blame, all frustration turns into a pumpkin.

⚭ *Forgiveness* ⚭

Faced with the choice between changing one's mind and proving there is no need to do so, almost everyone gets busy on the proof.

—economist John Kenneth Galbraith

With six billion people in the world, we might as well get along. That means forgiving one another. A poignant example of forgiveness is the coming of age of South Africa. In this country, the dark skinned majority was totally subservient to the light skinned minority. And there was total segregation. Then overnight, the tables turned. A total revolution. And miraculously, a peaceful revolution where bloodbath had been foreseen by all.

Archbishop and Nobel Peace Prize earner Desmond Tutu explains, "Instead of revenge and retribution, this new nation chose to tread the difficult path of confession, forgiveness, and reconciliation." He lists dozens of individual and collective acts of forgiveness and then adds, "Without forgiveness, there is no future." Countless South Africans moved their stones.

Without forgiveness there is no future. Can you be happy without a future, mired in the bogs of blame? Phan Thi Kim Phuc, better known as "the girl in the picture," shows how to forgive. You've probably seen her, the naked, screaming girl fleeing from a napalm attack in Vietnam. The photograph, possibly the most famous ever, was the icon for anti-war crusaders. In the most recent photo I saw of her, she is hugging John Plummer, the man who ordered that napalm attack. Phan Thi moved her stones.

Christianity is based on forgiveness. Forgiveness of original sin. Forgiveness of those who crucified Jesus. Forgiveness of those who hurt us. Most religious traditions rate forgiveness high among those virtues we should pursue.

When our religious leaders tell us to "forgive thy enemies," it's not for the sake of our enemies. Why should they care? With hate in our hearts we can be neither good nor happy. As the kids in the schoolyard used to say, when you point your finger, three fingers point back at you. It's the forgiver that benefits. Studies show that forgiving improves both physical and mental well-being.

Remember Terry Anderson, the American held hostage by the Islamic fundamentalist Hezbollah for six years? When he was released, he focused on the joy of his family reunion, rather than on bitterness against his captors. Terry moved his stones. He created happiness from within.

You might have heard that the best way to destroy an enemy is to turn him into a friend. That's what Steven Page of the Barenaked Ladies (the band, not strippers) discovered at a concert in Chicago. "It was like all these rock guys who called me faggot in high school…For us to get them singing along really was a case of revenge of the nerds." Go ahead and forgive. Your enemies will love you for it.

Sometimes it helps to place yourself in the other person's shoes. Why did he do that to you? Did he do it to you, or were you just in the way at the time? What pressure was the other person under? How might I have reacted in his shoes? What might I have done? This kind of empathy is not easy when someone has just destroyed your hope of ever landing that once-in a lifetime job you've plotted to nab for three years now. But empathy helps you forgive and get past the hurt feelings.

Forgiveness takes the high road. It says, "Whether you've done something wrong is irrelevant. I won't hold it against you." The sun shines longer on the mountain trail than on the path in the gully—which Bray Goat will appreciate when he escapes the well. And fewer rocks and stones fall on the high road than on the low road, which Sarah Sheep will appreciate when she escapes the well. Take the sunny high road of forgiveness, rather than the painful low road of grudges.

Forgiving others does not mean blaming yourself. Blame is not something that must be assigned. Blame looks backward to pain, instead of forward to gain. No pain, all gain. No gain, all pain. In the game of pin-the-blame-on-the-donkey, forgiveness removes the blindfold.

Exercise:
At whom are you upset? How can you forgive them? Make your plan today. Maybe it won't be easy, but it is possible and is in *your* best interest to do so.

There is a corollary to forgiving. It's apologizing, or in other words, seeking forgiveness from others. Admitting we've hurt someone, saying we're sorry, asking forgiveness is often the first step to rebuilding a damaged relationship. It allows us to forgive ourselves.

Three hundred Maryland criminals serving time volunteered to seek forgiveness from their victims face-to-face. The only incentive given was their desire to do so. Only one of the 300 was arrested again after his release. Forgiveness is a powerful motivator.

Three teens shot pellets into North Carolina runner Dan Hyde while they were target-practicing—a stupid thing to do, but not a malicious one. They called Hyde up to apologize, and he invited them out for a run six days later in the park where the shooting occurred. Because three people sought forgiveness and one granted it, all four healed much faster. Ask for forgiveness of anyone you might have wronged. You can't control that person's response—that's a dew stone, but by golly, you sure can ask—that's a multiple-choice stone. Most of all, don't forget to forgive yourself.

Apologizing allows others to forgive us and move on with their lives.

∞ *Don't look back* ∞

*Right now you hate yourself 'cause you knew better
But there's no use crying over spilled perfume.*

—singer Pam Tillis in "Spilled Perfume"

Imagine playing in a football game. Instead of running forward with the ball, you run backward. That's just what Roy "Wrong Way" Riegels did in 1929. He played for the University of California at Berkeley. Recovering the ball from a Georgia Tech fumble, Riegels ran with it for a touchdown. But he headed the wrong way. Teammate Benny Lom chased him all the way back to the California goal line screaming and hollering to him.

Benny tackled Wrong Way just six inches from the goal line, but Georgia Tech scored two points on the next play, winning the game 8 to 7. Run backward and you lose. Go forward and you win.

In Venice, Chantal and I put our forward vision and David's Incredible Time Machine to the test. We stayed at a lovely *pensione* in Lido called Hotel Stella. Despite its old-world charm, we would not recommend it to our fondest enemies.

The owner (let's call her the Wicked Witch) had just charged us our weight in lira for laundry she promised would dry in the fresh Italian breeze. Instead, she plopped down three plastic bags stuffed like turkeys with our crumpled clothes—our crumpled, damp clothes.

Chantal and I took turns trying to reason with her. We even asked to borrow the iron. "This is not a service we provide." Apparently, for another sack of gold she would graciously iron our wardrobe—even the wrinkle-free items that never needed ironing before.

Finally, "If you don't like, you can go to another hotel." And we almost did. Then we took stock: half a day (of our three days in Venice) hotel-hunting, packing our damp clothes, forfeiting some of our hefty hotel deposit, and still fuming about Wicked Witch Stella.

No. We chose to let it roll off our backs. Ten years later we wanted to remember the excitement of Venice, not the Wicked Witch's larceny. She could have spoiled our visit to Venice...but only if we had let her.

Another reason to release the past is that times change. People change. You change. We harbor anger, resentment, guilt, and blame long after the event has passed and the perpetrator has reformed or forgotten.

Times change and so do people. Our reactions should, too. It's one thing to be angry. It's another thing to hold on. The past is past. Cut it loose. Let it drift on the wings of time.

Another way to look at the past is the way good entrepreneurs do. They base decisions on probable outcomes. Sunk costs—anything already spent—must be ignored to make a sound business decision. Past pain, past anger, past guilt—these are sunk costs. In our personal lives we also have to make decisions based on probable outcomes. Our only choices lie ahead.

When you get to a fork in the road, take it. LauraKate Van Hollebeke of Seattle did. Tired of unfulfilling sexual relationships, she simply started over...and founded Born Again Virgins of America. (No, you don't have to go to such extremes.)

In Chapter 5, we learned about positive illusions, the healthy mind's ability to distort reality so as to enhance self-esteem, maintain a sense of control, and envisage an optimistic future. Better known as seeing the world through rose-colored glasses, positive illusions dispense with feelings of anger, pain, and guilt (or seeing the world through thorn-rimmed glasses).

Other psychological tools most people use are counterfactuals. Sometimes we use them to boost our morale. Other times we use them to rip apart our morale. Counterfactuals are statements that run counter to the facts (as if that isn't obvious): "could've been" and "would've been" and "if only."

"The plus side is that the disease is not contagious—which allows males to kiss our favorite women and vice versa," notes former *Ottawa*

Citizen editor and current Alzheimer's patient Christopher Young. That's a just-past-the-post counterfactual—it could've been worse, at least I made it.

"If only I'd gone to the dinner, I'd have met the mayor. If only I'd met the mayor, I'd have won the contract. If only I'd won the contract, I'd be rich. If only I was rich…" That's a just-missed-the-post counterfactual—if only it was better, too bad I didn't make it.

Studies show that shifting our thoughts from "what might have been" to "what might be" reduces feelings of guilt and regret. Remember our discussions about explanatory style in the previous two chapters? An internal explanatory style says, "It's my fault." The counterfactual thought is, "If only I hadn't been such a doofus." But we can turn that around with a positive counterfactual such as, "At least I got some of it right." Suddenly it's not all our fault. We mess some up, but we get some right.

So if you were gunning for that promotion, and it goes to someone else, move beyond your disappointment. Switch from, "I knew I wouldn't get it" and "Why didn't I get it?" to "Some day I'll get another chance" and "How can I bag the next one?" Not only will you feel better about the immediate situation, you will more likely succeed next time.

People around the world find ways to go past brooding, resolve problems, improve their situation. More than 6,000 residents of Huntington Beach, California, signed up as beach patrollers to avert a safety- and health-related beach closure. In Pennsbury Township, Pennsylvania, 80 Town Watch volunteers patrol to keep crime from sprouting in their community. You probably know people in your town who've banded together to exorcise some evil spirit haunting the community.

POP QUIZ:
Have you ever had trouble drowning a spider in the bath-tub? Down the drain in goes. Sllurrrrrp. But the next day, there it is again. How does it do that? Are spiders magic?
ANSWER: When you turn on the water, it instinctively curls up, trapping a bubble of air between its body and its legs. If the spider is not washed past the u-bend, it floats up to the surface, and climbs back into the tub. A spider might seem like an odd role model, but try to follow its example. Wrap yourself around a buoyant bubble of joy. Sure, you'll get washed down the drain from time to time, but you can always float back up.

Life is more than an endless post-mortem. Life is now. Learn what the past can teach, then move forward, float upward.

Keep your eyes on the road ahead

I demolish my bridges behind me...
then there is no choice but forward.

—Norwegian polar explorer Firdtjof Nansen

The past is over. There's really no point looking back. In the words of Elvis Presley, "You just forget the past, the future looks bright ahead." Simba, the Lion King, learns the same lesson: *hakuna matata.*

Make decisions to carry you toward fulfillment. Moving cross-country to start up a new career is an obvious example of this. My friend, Silvana, headed to California; my brother, Joel, worked in France; my high school buddy, Josh, headed to Israel; and half my Montreal high school class seems to have spent at least some time working in Europe, Asia, California, or Alberta.

When you drive along the road and see the blacktop right in front of you, do you ever notice how many cracks and potholes appear? But look ahead several yards, and the surface looks smooth. When Chantal or I see the other mucking around in frustration, we often call on David's Incredible Time Machine: "Will it matter in 10 years? Or even in six months?" Of course, the answer is invariably, "No." Put in perspective, all those irritants, all those daily wrinkles, all the potholes and cracks along our path disappear when we look farther down the road.

ᗍ *Move the stones* ᗍ

Out of the ashes, alive and free
No longer a slave to a memory
Got the rest of my life right out in front of me.

—country band Blackhawk in "Like there ain't no yesterday"

Move the stones, don't throw them. We all make mistakes, we all live in glass houses. If someone throws a stone at us or we throw it at her, either way, the house shatters, our happiness collapses, our yayism withers.

Throughout this book, we visit people who move their multiple-choice stones from the Great Wall of Misery to their Stairway to Heaven by how they react to situations. Some of these stonemasons move heavier stones than others, stones that require shaking off the past and following Yogi Berra down the fork in the road.

At age 16, Doris Day headed to New York City to dance on Broadway. She had sacrificed much of her youth for this big break. On the way, her car crashed, and the doctor told her she might never walk again. She never danced again, but she did walk. She had two choices: brood over her lost dancing legs, or forge a new path ahead. She moved forward and became a popular singer and actress of the 1950s. Doris moved her stones.

The arid Chilean mountain village of Caleta Chungungo had no source of water and virtually no rainfall. The village was literally drying up. Then someone "discovered" the town's most valuable asset: a low-lying cloud that passes by almost every night. They placed 86 nylon-mesh billboards to catch tiny droplets of water from the clouds. A single mesh collects up to 150 gallons of water in a night. Now everyone in the village is happier…and much less thirsty. The entire village moved its stones.

Once again, it comes down to who is in control. In Chapter 5, we asked: "Who runs your life?" Are you the victim of events or the victor over them? In Chapter 7, we asked: "Who paints your portrait?" Who defines you? In Chapter 9, we asked if you label the little things in your life "miracles" or "drudgery."

Now we ask you to decide who controls your reactions. This is a tough one. Nobody I know controls his or her reactions all the time. But some people rarely get upset. Some people don't hold grudges. We can't control what others do, but we do control how we react. And that determines how happy we will be from moment to moment.

Exercise:
Envisage what your road ahead looks like, tastes like, feels like without the burden of painful memories. See yourself moving on to positive goals you want to accomplish.

HABIT # 5

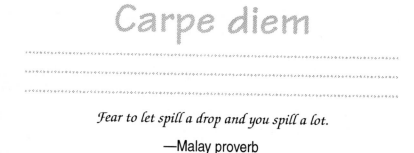

Carpe diem

Fear to let spill a drop and you spill a lot.

—Malay proverb

Carpe diem. If you think you know a little Latin, the title of this habit means, "Give us this day our daily fish." If you know more than a little Latin, you know it really means, "Seize the day." Not surprisingly, *Carpe Diem* is also the title of the Secret Society of Happy People's newsletter. *Carpe Diem* tells us we find happiness in action, not inaction.

Why not seize the day? What could stop us? Whatifism, that's what. What if she slaps my face? What if I fall? What if my mind goes blank? It's standing room only for whatifisms.

Whatifisms can paralyze us. They can also spur us to action. What if, hiding in the shadows, we miss the opportunity of a lifetime? What if the Scarecrow, and the Tin Man, and the Cowardly Lion had been overcome with whatifism? What if I never write this book? What if it's dangerous out there? Yeah, but what if it's worse in here?

POP QUIZ:
What's the secret to success?

ANSWER: When Purdue University President Steven Beering was asked what one book would guarantee any college graduate a successful career, he named *The Little Engine That Could.*

Research shows that what we are willing to risk heading forward depends on what we see in the ripples behind us. Those ripples define our Comfort Zone. If you don't take some risks, step out of your Comfort Zone, do what you've been dying to do, you might never find out "What if?" What if you spend the rest of your life wondering, "What if?" That's not the recipe for happiness. In this chapter, let's *carpe diem*. Let's update to a state-of-the-heart life by replacing "What if?" with "That's what!"

CHAPTER 13

Hiding in the casket

Fear makes the wolf bigger than he is.

—German proverb

In my media relations seminars, I explain the traps that grab some people when speaking to the media, and I offer ways to avoid those traps. Knowing that I speak to the media more than 600 times a year, one lady asked me, "How do you sleep at night?" I hadn't thought about it like that before. I simply do my job, I enjoy it, and when something doesn't go as planned, I deal with it. If I followed the premise of her question, that speaking to the media could send even the Sandman scurrying in retreat, my career as a consumer advocate would be miserable. (And it's not.)

I enjoy speaking with live audiences even more than speaking with the media. I enjoy the feedback, the social contact, the face-to-face communication. Believe it or not, more people are afraid of speaking in front of an audience than of dying. In my speaking seminars, I interpret this for participants: "At a funeral, people would rather be in the casket than delivering the eulogy."

New York writer Anne Bernays, who played piano in her youth, says, "My most recurrent anxiety dream is not about writing but about getting up onstage and realizing I haven't learned my solo."

My first foray into public speaking was as class representative on my high school student council. With the class gathered 'round, I reported on student council meetings from a raised stool. I kept tossing my head back, as if to remove a bothersome lock of hair. Just one problem…my hair was not hanging in my face. If only someone had spoken up and said, "Why are you doing that? There's no hair in your face," I would have stopped. But my classmates were too polite, and I continued to make a fool of myself. (And I know I'm probably the only one in the class who remembers this.)

I know two people who joined Toastmasters to conquer their stutters. The first not only conquered his stutter, but went on to reach the highest Toastmaster ranks. Bravo! The second is just starting out. Best of luck! Having conquered my own fear of speaking, I no longer try to toss imaginary hair. Now I love the energy a public platform builds in me.

POP QUIZ:
How can you get rid of butterflies in your stomach—you know, the ones stomping around in there with their 12-pound army boots?
ANSWER: You can't. And you shouldn't. The butterflies are your energy, your driving force. They help you focus…when they fly in formation. And they will, if you focus on your audience/prospect/object of adoration/whomever you're speaking with, rather than on yourself.

∞ *What, me worry?* ∞

There is no terror in the bang, only in the anticipation of it.

—film producer Alfred Hitchcock

When your heart beats, that's a good sign. It means you're alive. But what about when it pounds, like it's ready to burst forth from your rib cage and bounce around the room in a panic-stricken frenzy? That's the terror Sarah Sheep feels as the stones keep falling and her limbs

> **What's to fear?**
>
> Chromophobia (fear of colors)
> Batophobia (fear of passing a tall building)
> Alektorophobia (fear of chickens)
> Teratophobia (fear of bearing a monster)
> Oikophobia (fear of home surroundings)

grow tired. What if she can't carry on? What if the stones keep falling? What if she's buried alive? Well, not alive for very long! The sheer terror of it energizes her.

The notion of fear might inspire images of vampires and witches, pain or darkness, wild animals or heights. Harvard psychology professor Jerome Kagan says that adult fears are mostly "anticipatory," such as fearing future relations with others, running the risk of criticism, performance in school and at work, social disruption.

We decide to act...and whatifism strikes! We doubt ourselves. We doubt others. We envisage the worst. We might even be afraid to admit fear.

It might help to review our previous lessons. Remember defining success in Chapter 2? Did you define it as impressing yourself or as impressing others? Do you think you'll impress yourself more if you try or if you don't ? In Chapter 4, we learned about spotmisserism and why we should cheer our successes, no matter how small. Impress yourself. *Carpe diem.*

Kakorrhaphiophobia (What if I fail?)

How very little can be done under the spirit of fear.

—wartime nursing heroine Florence Nightingale

If you can pronounce kakorrhaphiophobia, throw a parade for yourself. It's got enough letters to fill a 10-gallon hat. Of course, not everybody who fears something or feels anxious about something has a phobia. Phobias are the extreme versions of fear. In this case, fear of failure.

Have you ever overstayed your own welcome? Most people do at some point. We stay put in a job that no longer inspires our minds. We remain with a partner who no longer inspires our hearts. Stuck in the Comfort Zone! We hate where we are. We don't feel happy. We don't feel inspired. But we somehow feel...comfortable. The Comfort Zone shields us from feeling kakorrhaphiophobia.

One Web designer decided he was tired of his employer's "enthusiastic micromanagement." But he was afraid to leave because he'd never quit a project before. It's easy to quit a job when another awaits. It's easy to leave a lover when another beckons. It's not so easy to leap into the void. What if I don't find something better? What if I don't find some-*one* better? The Comfort Zone is jam-packed with whatifisms.

Vince and Karen, friends of ours, leaped over their whatifisms. They both wanted a career change, and they both had to relocate to fulfill their dreams. So they did. They saved a buck or two and, no job offer in hand, hit the road. They moved their stones.

Exercise:
Define your Comfort Zone. Are there things, big or small, that you want to change? Write them down now.

Maybe we don't always fear failure. Maybe we simply fear that others will see us as a failure. Are we afraid of being judged? Do we turn to The Mask of Success to shield us from the pain of failure in others' eyes?

If you expect very little, you'll get lots of it. If you try for lots, you might just get some of it. Every risk we take is a success, even if we wonder how others might view it. Sometimes just showing up counts. When you *carpe diem*, you cannot fail.

∞ **Glossophobia (What if I don't know what to say?)** ∞

Happiness hates the timid.

—playwright Eugene O'Neil

Some people are genuinely shy…right across the board. Violet is one of those people. She averts her eyes. She hopes she won't be called upon to speak. Shrinking Violet thinks she's the only one who's shy. One of the scariest things about shyness is the feeling of isolation. Indiana psychologist Bernardo Carducci says that almost half the population is shy. Half the people in a crowded room are thinking, "I'm the only shy person in this room."

POP QUIZ: ....

What terrifies Shrinking Violet the most?

ANSWER: Researchers identify three typical situations that bring anxiety to the shy person's heart: interaction with authorities and strangers, one-on-one opposite sex interactions, and unstructured social settings. Boy, does that sound like me! After years of work, these situations no longer breed anxiety in me…but I'm not always comfortable either.

The simple act of speaking to a stranger might seem to many of us—not just to Shrinking Violet—like swimming with sharks. How often do you strike up a conversation with someone in an elevator? Or in the supermarket checkout line? Or in a waiting room? If you're like most people, you don't talk to strangers…and you even avert your eyes so they won't speak to you.

As silly as it sounds, we usually press our mute button in the company of strangers. It might simply be that our parents told us, "Don't talk to strangers," and we learn the lesson better than they planned. What do we miss that way? I've had some delightful conversations with strangers in supermarket checkout lines, in airports, in hotel lobbies. My only regret is that I so infrequently take the risk. My personal resolution is to take that risk more often.

My brother, Joel, tells about the time he saw a woman enter a pharmacy, leaving her full grocery cart on the strip mall sidewalk. As he approached, another lady was passing by. She looked at my brother and said, "I'm sorry, but I want to say something." Imagine that—she actually apologized for speaking to him! "That woman who just left the cart full of groceries is very trusting," she continued. "Especially in today's world." Joel agreed, they chatted a few moments, then they each went their way. She moved her stones, but my brother was surprised that she felt the need to apologize first.

In today's alienated world, reaching out to someone we don't know takes nerves of steel. The lady's need to apologize reveals how very much of a risk she felt she was taking—how very little trust she felt she could place in a stranger.

Chantal and I visited Sienna, Italy, on our honeymoon. Left alone while Chantal searched for the elusive public restroom, I saw a young couple taking turns with the camera. Knowing how we value having photos with both of us *together*, I offered to snap their picture. I can't begin to describe how grateful they were. It turns out they were on their honeymoon, too. But they were too shy to approach a stranger to take their picture. If I had not offered, their honeymoon album would not have included a single picture of them together.

At least the shy couple in Sienna had each other. Eighty-three percent of men and 76 percent of women express anxiety about asking someone for a date. The single shy guy walks the plank daily. (I'm sure glad that's not me...anymore.) But dating is a subject worthy of its own book, and I know better than to try and write it.

Social events test Shrinking Violet's mettle. The dinner party, the cocktail reception, the church picnic—any time casual conversation or small talk is called for. Actress Nicole Kidman describes how, "I can still get very, very shy. It used to tick Tom (Cruise) off. We'd go to a dinner party and I'd hardly speak. He didn't understand it."

Chimpanzee expert Jane Goodall found a way to break through the artificial chitchat of social functions. At a meeting in Beijing, she broke the ice by greeting top level officials with a heavy breathing "huh-huh-huh" sound. She then informed her startled hosts that this "is the way any self-respecting female chimp greets a high-ranking male." Now that took guts.

In olden days, casual conversation was a part of everyday life. We'd chat with the butcher and the bank teller. Now, when I answer the phone, it's not uncommon to hear the surprised caller exclaim, "Oh, I thought I'd get your voice mail." At this rate, our vocal chords will devolve right out of existence in a few generations.

People with good social skills are likely to be happier. Whether on an elevator, at a social function, in the grocery checkout line, or in a bar, it's not that hard to strike up a conversation. "Nice tie," will do it. "Will it ever stop raining?" works. "Did you hear they were going to raise parking fees?" will elicit a good response.

> **Exercise:**
>
> **Part I:** Write down 10 interesting things about yourself and your interests—10 things you feel comfortable sharing with others. You might want to include a vacation at Cape Cod, a job you had while studying at college, or a strange neighbor you used to know.
>
> **Part II:** Write down 10 questions you could ask a stranger you meet at a social event. Don't include questions about sexual preferences or entomology, and stay away from politics, religion, and digestive practices. You might want to ask questions that allow the other person to talk about herself. The first step to being a good conversationalist is to be a good listener. But why not pick topics you, too, can speak on…like, "Where are you from?" or "How was your summer?" Go ahead, make your list.

∞ *Paranoia (What if the world is out to get me?)* ∞

A ship in port is safe, but that is not what ships are for.
Sail out to sea and do new things.

—American rear admiral "Amazing Grace" Hopper

The doctor stood up and announced to the anxious couple, "I can hear three hearts."

"You mean we're so nervous you can hear our hearts beat, too?" the husband asked.

"No," the doctor said. "I mean I can hear three hearts in your wife's tummy. Congratulations...it's triplets."

"In that case," the woman declared with a tense glance at her husband. "You better make that five hearts, 'cause ours are beating the loudest."

A coward dies a thousand deaths. If we don't choose to live, we die by default. We hide in the casket.

POP QUIZ:

Who is that you see in the distance, the bogeyman or the boogyman?

ANSWER: If you fear him, he's the bogeyman...no matter who he is.

Fear of the unknown is pessimism. Think about it. Something unknown could be good or bad, lucky or unlucky, welcome or unwelcome. The unknown could be Noah's arc, teeming with life, packed with excitement. Or it could be a Trojan horse, stuffed with hungry saber-toothed tigers lying in ambush. Why choose to fear? We could just as easily choose to cheer. Being hopeful—but careful—is cautious optimism (and possibly the best compromise between happiness and not being eaten).

Stress breeds fear. Philip Gold, a psychologist with the National Institute of Mental Health, reports that stress helps people survive in immediate, threatening situations. But their lives are less comfortable. Remember Miles, the producer in *Murphy Brown*? Always stressed, always on guard, never in truly threatening situations. Given that few saber-toothed tigers roam the streets of Detroit or the beaches of North Carolina, wouldn't we all be better off with less fear?

Low-income people suffer more anxiety, more phobias, more worry. Remember how money does not buy happiness, but its absence breeds misery. Low-income people worry more about holding a job. They worry more about family debt. They worry more about walking the streets in their poor, urban neighborhoods. Worry breeds fear.

An Australian study found that fear of burglaries greatly diminishes life satisfaction. When our safe haven isn't so safe, life becomes a very scary ordeal. Nurses in Silver Springs, Maryland, learned this lesson. They were flipping channels on an office TV. When they flipped to Channel 16, they were shocked to be watching *Nurse's Dressing Room Live*. They had no idea they had to fear Peeping Toms, but I wonder if paranoia haunts them still.

∞ *Topophobia (What if I freeze?)* ∞

The crisis of today is the joke of tomorrow.

—science fiction writer H.G. Wells

Hopefully you've never seen the deer-in-the-headlights look. You're driving along, and suddenly up ahead you see a deer in your path. For me, it was a porcupine. Instead of running for cover, the deer (or porcupine) freezes in mid-road, overcome by unbridled inertia. If you love animals as much as I do, it's a terrifying sight. If you love people, it's equally sad to watch them freeze in mid-life.

I remember taking my mother back to Hungary, where she grew up. It was shortly after the fall of the Berlin Wall. Meanwhile, over in Moscow, the hard-line Communists tried to recapture the Soviet Union. People around the world were glued to images of Boris Yeltsin standing up to the tanks outside the Kremlin, while Mikhail Gorbachev sat imprisoned in his Ukraine villa.

In Budapest, most of the westerners imprisoned themselves in their hotels, huddled next to the radio, visions of evil Russian soldiers stomping in their heads. My mother, as a fugitive from the Communists so long ago, had more reason to be afraid than any of them. So what did we do? We hopped in our rental car and drove around the country-side…just as we had planned. We were not about to let fear ruin our trip.

Fear won't hurt you if you don't let it hold you back. Unfortunately, fear is often a self-fulfilling prophecy. Small talk is not my forte. Many a time I've gone to a reception or party nervous about having to make small talk, afraid of being sidelined. The result? I would withhold comments and—you guessed it—sideline myself.

Even world rulers—bigwig company directors—freeze in the headlights. *The Economist* magazine offers this insight: "Confronted with a chief executive whose strategy is not working, the instinct of many company directors is to wait in the hope that something—the shares, ideally—will turn up. Far better to find a replacement, quickly, and pay the price."

Are you afraid of heights? Can you climb your Stairway if you're afraid? Of course not. Fear is natural. Fear enables us to elude the saber-toothed tiger. But with so few saber-toothed tigers left (just a few, I'm told, working as tax collectors), it's time to renounce fear, stage fright, headlights.

Of course we can always find excuses to avoid doing something. Remember, "My dog ate my homework"? After a while our dogs knew more than we did. Or how about, "My canary died"? (Should have chosen a cat. That excuse is good for nine times.) Maybe now you say, "I haven't got time." Or, "I haven't any money."

It all comes down to priorities. The same people who don't have time or money often spend that time in front of a 693-inch television screen they bought with the extra money they don't have. The question each of us has to ask is how to allocate our time, our money, our efforts.

Exercise: ....
Remember your Comfort Zone? Are you immobilized when you step out of it? What steps could you take to get moving? Write down ways to keep yourself moving beyond the bounds of your Comfort Zone.

If all the world's a stage, now is no time for stage fright. Lights, camera, action. It's time to climb out of the casket, out of the Comfort Zone, onto the stage, and do what you've always wanted to do.

CHAPTER 14

Do what you want to do

Mañana is often the busiest day of the week.

—Spanish proverb

It's time to make a life-and-death decision. Will you do what you've always wanted to do? Will you really live? Or will you die by default? Only dead people hide in the casket, and I'm sure you don't want to condemn yourself to death before your time. Arise! Get ready to live.

Chantal's mother wanted to spend some of her vacation with us. It just so happened that we were camping for a few days at that time. She had never camped and had no interest in sleeping on the ground or in a bear's backyard. Nonetheless, she stepped out of her Comfort Zone and into our campsite (and she plans to do it again). Yay!

POP QUIZ:

Why do you do what you do? Because it fulfills you? Or because it will please your parents or earn you brownie points or fit in to what you think others expect of you?

Do what you want to do because it fulfills you. That's the only good reason. When your job ceases to fulfill you, plan your escape and make your break. Country singer Lee Ann Womack remembers her high school guidance counselor's reaction when she wrote "country singer" on his career questionnaire: "He wanted me to pick something from the chart, and then, as a hobby, I could sing at weddings."

Calista Flockhart explains why she risked her career for an obscure play instead of staying in the limelight of TV and the movies: "There was no strategy involved. I decided I really wanted to do a play, and I was fascinated by the material." Joan Brett knew during her second day of cooking school in New York that she wanted to open one in her hometown of Boulder, Colorado. And she did.

My parents, several years retired now, are part-time university students. Not a term goes by without a class. Never mind the room full of "kids"…this is what they want to do. It's never too late to go back to school. Colonel Harland Sanders started building his Kentucky Fried Chicken empire at age 65. Apparently, it's never too late to fry a chicken either.

These people chose to paint their own portraits. And they all took risks or overcame fears to follow their dreams. They picked up the scary stones from the Great Wall of Misery and plunked them down on their Stairway to Heaven.

Don't cancel your parade due to a rain of terror. You can overcome fear and do what you really want.

∞ *The difference between courage and stupidity* ∞

Wanted, Alligator wrestlers.
Must be brave and a risk taker.
Males and females OK. No experience needed.

—job posting in Hollywood, Florida

If you can stay calm, while all around you is chaos...then you probably haven't grasped the gravity of the situation. That's right, sometimes a little fear is good medicine. Please don't mistake this chapter for a road-kill-in-training license.

There's a fine line between courage and stupidity. That's the line Sir Francis Bacon crossed when, in the name of science, he ate a goose stuffed with snow. Would the cold repulse the meat's natural decay, he wondered? Nope. He died of typhoid and has remained dead ever since. Winning a bet that he wouldn't place a revolver in his mouth did not make Delaware resident Sylvester Briddell, Jr. courageous. It made him dead.

Little Cindy was no Shrinking Violet. She took her bike for a ride around the block. As she passed her house, she cried out, "Look, Ma, no hands." And around the block she rode, until she passed her house again and shouted, "Look, Ma, no hands, no feet." And around the block she rode once more, until she passed her house again and shouted, "Look, Ma, no hands, no feet, no teeth." She could have added, "Look, Ma, no brains."

Here are a few things I do not recommend you risking (I call them stupid people tricks): the running of the bulls in Pamplona (Try instead the "running of the sheep" in Reed Point, Montana. It's much safer.); parachuting from a skyscraper, as one fool tried from Cincinnati's Carew Tower, before getting stuck on the way down; staring down firecracker launching tubes, as one Long Islander did (may he rest in peace); or taking a shortcut under a slow-moving train, which cost one Illinois lady her toes.

Despite legitimate risks, people keep moving to the coasts. Each year, 1,500 coastal homes in the United States will be lost to erosion at a cost of $530 million a year. People continue to build in flood plains, despite higher insurance rates. Among the fastest-growing areas in the United States are the southwest deserts, where water will sooner or later run dry. Many people will take calculated risks when they want something enough.

Just make sure the calculations are accurate.

What's the real risk?

*To a certain extent,
a little blindness is necessary when you undertake a risk.*

—Microsoft founder Bill Gates

Around the world, since the beginning of time, people have feared snakes and spiders. Satan himself is portrayed as a snake in the Bible. Greater dangers—such as alcohol, tobacco, not wearing a seatbelt, saturated fats, couch potatohood, toxic waste, knives or guns in the home, wireless-world radiation, and terrorists developing planet-consuming biological weapons—elicit a calmer reaction. But snakes scare people.

The *Smithsonian* magazine writes, "Everywhere in France—in potato fields and orchards, under town squares and back porches—the fallout from two world wars has turned the national soil into an enormous booby trap." That doesn't stop locals or tourists from flitting about with no worries of becoming human popcorn.

We delay our visit to the dentist to avoid pain. In the end, we endure greater pain and maybe the loss of a tooth. Afraid of the repercussions, we avoid disagreeing with the boss, even though we know his decision means we'll slave for nothing…and we'll have to redo the work later rather than sooner (not to mention grumbling all the way). We tell our children not to talk to strangers, depriving them of a healthy psychological development, but we don't tell them to stay away from people they know or to keep out of cars, both of which are much greater risk to their safety.

POP QUIZ:
Why did one Detroit legislator propose a ban of Super Soaker® water guns, but oppose any control of real (lethal) guns?
ANSWER: Who knows?

All through history, we've measured risk. Noah had to ask whether it was worth the risk to build his big boat. (It was.) Napoleon had to decide if it was worth the risk to invade Russia. (It was not.) We had to figure out if it was worth the risk to legalize cell phones with funny sounding rings. (We're not sure.)

Here's the lowdown on what we face on the street:

- In the words of *Smithsonian* senior editor John Ross, "We spend a billion dollars to tamperproof packaging when seven people die from poisoned Tylenol tablets, yet we do nothing about the fifty children who drown every year in 5-gallon buckets."
- Lightening kills three times as many people as violence in schools. Virginia park ranger Roy Sullivan, the Human Lightening Rod, attracted lightening seven times in 35 years. The bolts relieved him of a toenail, his eyebrows, and his hair. If lightening picks you to strike, you run a one-in-four risk of dying. But people fear school violence more.
- Beds, mattresses, and pillows injure 400,000 Americans every year.
- Perrier recalled 72 million bottles of water in 1990 because a trace of benzene was discovered in some bottles. The additional risk of cancer was no more than one in 100,000...if you drink four cups each day for the rest of your life. By comparison, living with a smoker kills one in 700 people (or 142 times as much risk).
- About 1,000 Americans die each day from smoking. The risk of dying from smoking a pack a day is one in six. Which begs a question: why is it Perrier that had to recall its product while cigarette manufacturers are free to sell theirs?

- Eating a peanut butter sandwich (yum!) is more hazardous to your health than living next door to a nuclear power plant for 5 years.
- An average number of x-rays kills one in 700 people. Presumably, they save many more lives than are lost.
- Heart disease is still the leading killer in America, even if the 11th-ranked cause—homicide—gets all the media attention.

Good grief! Are we scaring ourselves to death? Hmmm, I wonder what's the risk of that…

We fear the wrong things. Sometimes we lack information, and sometimes the Merchants of Misery feed us false fear. (Please. They like to call it "selective information.") If we fear "ring around the collar," we'll buy a cleansing product. If we fear alar on our apples, we'll oppose pesticides. If we fear burglaries, we'll buy a gun. Whatever a company's or interest group's agenda, fear is a powerful tool, and we are pliable targets.

Exercise:
For each project you would like to do beyond your Comfort Zone, write down the risk. Is it too big? Is it a stupid risk to take? Can you handle it? Do you know what the true risk is?

Find out what the true risks are before scaring yourself to death over something that might not be all that scary.

⨉ *Couldov beans* ⨉

A person who regrets marrying Mr. Wrong will likely get divorced;
someone who regrets passing up Mr. Right
typically must cope with the fact that he is no longer available.

—Cornell psychology professors Thomas Gilovich and Victoria Hasted Medvec

The farmer grows green beans, pole beans, wax beans, even fava beans. The fearer grows couldov beans. When we stock up on what ifs, we end up with could've beens. We grow so many couldov beans that Michigan psychologist Janet Landman reports regret is the second most common emotion we talk about.

We are twice as likely to regret inaction as we are to regret our actions. In one experiment, 77 people named 213 of their biggest regrets: 128 failures to act, 75 actions, and 10 events out of their control. As Australian psychologist Steven Baum puts it, "If actions speak louder than words, they also cause less regret."

What do people regret most? Failure to self actualize–not pursuing education or career, not developing a talent, not adequately fulfilling one's role as a parent, not being more assertive. We find ourselves asking, "Why didn't I at least give it a shot?"

Killing time is not a victimless crime. Time for each of us is finite, and when we kill time, we also kill dreams, opportunities, maybe even life itself. Septuagenarian Fred Reynolds typifies this. He regrets not having learned to swim, taken singing lessons ("When I have time and money"), learned Spanish, or decided whether or not there is a God.

Most people replay the video of their lives wishing they had taken more risks. Jack traded his cow for a handful of couldov beans. But he took the risk and planted them before it was too late. Psychologists in Michigan and Texas studied three groups of mature women: those with no regrets earlier in life, those who made life changes to thwart early regret, and those who did not respond to early regret. You guessed it, those with regret who made no changes earlier in life measure lower than the others in later well-being.

Let's do a quick reality check. Nobody on his deathbed has been known to say, "I wish I'd spent more time at the office," or, "I wish I had mowed the lawn more or cleaned the bathroom more or watched more television on that 693-inch screen I bought in Chapter 13." These are all things we have to do—work, clean, escape, shop—but they are not the things that bring us happiness.

Exercise:

Let's stir the pot a bit. Think about all your couldov beans—all the things you would really like to have done. Are there any you could still do? No excuses, now. To help you with all the things you would like to do, think of all the things you do now that you would never regret doing less of, like spending time at the office, mowing, cleaning, watching TV, and shopping. For each one, try to rearrange your life to spend less time. Remember, time is finite; how you use it is up to you. If you can spend less time doing the chores of life, you can spend more time doing those things  you've always wanted to do. The time is now to plan anything you might later regret not having done. This is far too important to put off "until I have some time" or "when I have the money."

Maybe when the **BOING!** of mid-life crisis strikes, it's not a crisis at all. Maybe the crisis is that we failed to take risks when we should have. Maybe we should call it "mid-life revival." After all, a steady diet of couldov beans won't make your golden years very golden. You can make the past better than it was going to be.

⌘ **Step outside the Comfort Zone** ⌘

Do an outrageous act every day.

—Manitoba Senator Mira Spivak

Do you hide behind the Mask of Success, afraid to paint your own portrait? Is a self-portrait the risk you would love to take? Bolsterism can help (see Chapter 9). In fact, you can bolster yourself.

Past experience might tell us this is a big, bad world. Somebody hurt us. We failed. People might not like us. The first four habits teach you to value yourself and what you do and what you have and—most importantly—to leave past pain behind. When you master the first four habits, the world is a much safer place for you to take a risk. That's why the habits are in this order. You bolster yourself with those habits.

Instead of the usual pre-wedding stag party for my brother, Aaron, we treated him to a whirlwind of activities, including whitewater rafting. What a thrill! Part way through, we parked the rafts and filed up a rocky path to a cliff some 12 feet above the rushing water. When my turn came, I couldn't jump into the gushing current below. I had jumped once from a rock almost that high…after an hour-and-a-half of courage building. But this water wasn't calm and beckoning. It was wild and threatening, and I was no Daredevil David. To this day, I don't know what I was afraid of, but whatifism got the better of me. Don't let that happen to you.

Like a turtle without its shell, Lady Godiva rode outside her Comfort Zone. Lady Dziewanna recently repeated the feat in Krakow, Poland, to protest high taxes. How many people are shy even to undress in the changing room at a swimming pool?

Kathrine Switzer broke out of the Comfort Zone when she registered for what was then the all-male Boston Marathon under the name of K.V. Switzer. Despite an attempted tackle by a marathon official, she completed the race. She moved her stones. No couldov beans on her menu.

POP QUIZ: ....
How do you boil a frog? (And why is an animal lover like me asking such a yucky question?)
ANSWER: If you toss a frog into boiling water—Yikes!—it jumps right out. It just won't boil. Place it in warm water and slowly—*veeerrrry* slowly—increase the heat. The frog adjusts—ribbit—to the temperature. It relaxes in the Comfort Zone. Even as the temperature slowly rises, the frog adjusts.

The Comfort Zone gets hotter, and the frog starts to cook. Remind you of anyone? The person who stays in a job that no longer inspires. Or the one who stays in a relationship that no longer fulfills. Even as the situation slowly worsens, our Comfort Zone adjusts, and we just ribbit along.

Tycoon Malcolm Forbes once said, "People who never get carried away should be." Let's not just ribbit in the Comfort Zone. You might not find the courage to step out every time. You might even choose not to, after calculating the risks. In fact, sometimes the Comfort Zone is just where you should be. But don't let the Comfort Zone hold you back. When you want to do something really important, rise to the challenge and jump out of the Comfort Zone.

⚭ *Dare to fear* ⚭

Fear is always with us, but we just don't have time for it. Not now.

—First Lady Hillary Rodham Clinton in her 1969 commencement address

Courage is not the opposite of fear. They are partners. You cannot be courageous if you are not afraid. Fairy tales tell of heroic knights who valiantly slay dreaded dragons. "Hold on yon maiden in distress. I'll rescue you. I'm not afraid." Well, if the knight is not afraid, it doesn't take much courage to fight the dragon, does it?

The Cowardly Lion was terrified of travelling to the Emerald City, but he overcame, or at least controlled, his fear and made the trip in spite of the danger. Did that take courage? You bet it did. He even got a medal in honor of his bravery.

Sometimes we have to overcome fear if we want to rise to the challenge, to *carpe diem*, to seize the day. As First Lady Nancy Reagan once said, "A woman is like a tea bag. You never know her strength until you drop her in hot water."

That's just what Sarah Sheep was thinking. No way will she be buried alive. Whatever her fears, whatever the risks, she knows she has two choices: live by her will or die by default. She just has to ignore her fear and keep stepping up. What a brave sheep!

The joy of overcoming fear

The happy individual's world seems to be one subjectively teeming with attractive possibilities.

—University of California psychology professor Sonja Lyubomirsky

I learned how fulfilling it is to overcome fear in grade school. I was supposed to "meet" feisty Howard Capstick after school. Now, I had felt Howard's punch, well honed on several of his older brothers, and a coward like me did not want to feel it again. I gulped down my fear and met Howard after school that day. Surprised that I even showed up, he decided we didn't have to fight after all. Whew!

Julie Noble hosted 60,000 guests, every one of the honeybee persuasion. They swarmed into her Dallas backyard, terrifying both her and her nine-year-old daughter. But honeybees are generally harmless, and these were *en route* to a more rural nesting ground. Bee experts helped them calculate the true risks. The Nobles decided to let the bees stay awhile—long enough to marvel. "I just tell everybody to get the camera. It's a once-in-a-lifetime experience."

Melody was 30 when she lost her husband. They dated in high school and married early. She was so scared to face the world all by herself. She retreated into her own little world, leaving the house only for work and groceries. It took her 20 years to overcome her fear—20 years of loneliness, 20 years of wishing, 20 years of whatifism. Until she decided to find out "what if." That's when she met her second husband. Dead at 30, married at 50.

Overcoming fear, rising to the challenge, leaping from the Comfort Zone is a fulfilling experience. I think that's why I enjoy Toastmasters meetings so much. Each person stepping out from the Comfort Zone. Each one taking a risk. Each one filling the room with positive energy. I glow after a Toastmasters meeting… even when I don't utter a peep.

You can live your life on cruise control, but you might regret never exploring any of the side roads. The next time you feel afraid or even just a little anxious about doing something, make the choice to leap out of your Comfort Zone. Just do it.

Exercise:

You know your Comfort Zone, you know what you want to do and the steps to take, you know the true risks involved. Now it's time to do it!

BREAK

SEVENTH HABIT STRETCH

HABITS # *6* AND # *7*

Slow it down, pump it up

Don't let worry kill you–let the church help.

—church bulletin blooper

Even the most successful baseball player stops playing for the seventh inning stretch. This short break happens three-quarters of the way through the game. It's a chance for players and audience alike to release tension and stretch their limbs.

Habits #6 and #7 are our seventh inning stretch. And how appropriate. These habits, although seemingly opposite, both help us reduce stress and other tensions that can keep us from maximum happiness. After breaking free from your Comfort Zone, you might feel stressed. After all, it takes a lot of energy to break free. So now's the time for our seventh inning stretch.

Stress reduces happiness. When we're on edge, tense, upset, worried, tired, we miss the joy we could be feeling. Stress also attacks our bodies, disarms our immune systems, and leads to several ailments. Those habitat stones are not in your Stairway. They make us grumpy and distance us from our support network.

POP QUIZ:
What good is stress?
ANSWER: Our flight-or-fight response to danger served us well when saber-toothed tigers were salivating over our tasty flesh. In the modern world, the stress our instincts create has no natural outlet. Stress builds. As it builds, our physical and psychological well-being is damaged. Let's see how we can tame the savage cave-person within...

CHAPTER 15

Stressed or rest

You can outdistance that which is running after you,
but not what is running inside you.

—Rwandan proverb

Life is 45 percent harder today than it was 35 years ago, say researchers at the University of Washington. Sigh.

Once upon a time, the gentry classes controlled the wealth. They lorded over their riches. They played. They snubbed the grimy masses who toiled 16-hour days for a meager portion of bread.

Times change. Now, almost everybody works in a sweatshop. In fact, the leaders, the executives, the managers are the ones who sneak into the office before rush hour and burn the midnight oil when day is (in theory) done. As *Fortune* magazine puts it, "The working class now has more leisure, and the leisure class now has more work." But we all seem to have more stress.

POP QUIZ:
How does stress affect your happiness?

ANSWER: Stress cripples our immune systems, shortening our lives. It damages our heart, leads to diabetes, disrupts the digestive system, leads to strokes, and reduces our mental capacities. A Harvard study found that 60 to 90 percent of visits to family physicians are stress-related. Worse, stress can lead to suicide. In 1996, 31,000 Americans committed suicide. Another 500,000 visited emergency rooms due to attempted suicide. These are not signs of happiness.

Stress comes both from external sources (illness, death, job loss, angry neighbor with chainsaw in his hand and evil glint in his eye, etc.) and internal sources (perfectionism, expectations, reactions to situations, etc.) Flashback to Chapter 1. Remember how we made that important distinction between the immobile foundation stones, the hard-to-move habitat stones, and the fleeting dew stones on the one hand, and the multiple-choice stones you can transfer from the Great Wall of Misery to your Stairway to Heaven?

External stress is difficult to change. You can move to another city to reduce stress. You can change jobs. You can alter family relationships. But those are all life-sized decisions and not part of this book. Internal stress can be managed on a day-to-day basis through—you guessed it—habits. That's what this chapter of the book is about.

⚭ *Octopus on duty* ⚭

The trouble with the rat race is that even if you win,
you're still a rat.

—comedienne Lily Tomlin

Fax, e-mail, voice mail, pager, in-box, photocopier, meetings, conferences, reports, cell phones—STOP! Imagine if Shakespeare or Freud or Mozart or Jefferson had all our modern time-saving gizmos. They never would have accomplished anything.

Do you feel like your job title should be Chief Octopus? Even though nine out of 10 Americans say they are at least somewhat satisfied with their jobs, two-thirds of them (and more than a third of Canadians) say their jobs are stressful. In September, when people return from vacation, and ties and scarves replace casual attire in the office, Pepto-Bismol sales jump. Welcome back.

The cell phone is the most pervasive symbol of octopitis. (Another entry in the Dictionary of David.) Your boss can reach you. Friends know where you are. As cell phones grow more sophisticated, the only person you won't find time for is you. Cell phones offer us the freedom of a wireless leash. The Merchants of Misery are jumping for joy; now they can pester us with advertisements everywhere we go.

No doubt, some of our impatient behaviors, like road rage and checkout line squabbles, are due to the stress of an overflowing agenda. A quarter of Americans say they see someone run a red light every day! Why so impatient? Why do we live just-in-time lives?

A reporter friend describes the fracas of a TV newsroom: "Some of the reporters get frazzled by the pressure. But you get so used to filing on deadline, you can't let it get to you." If it wasn't for the last minute, nothing would get done. We live our lives trying to outrun one deadline after the other. And one by one, they each *whhooooshh* on by.

In Chapter 2, we saw the difference between climbing the career ladder and climbing your Stairway to Heaven. From the world of animals, we find another difference. The dominant animal atop the pecking order packs the most cortisol. Cortisol is a stress hormone. The stress of keeping the other baboons, wild dogs, and mongooses subservient grinds down the pack leaders. As Secretary of State Henry Kissinger once remarked, "There can't be a crisis next week. My schedule is already full."

"I'd like to redesign my job so that I work a 32-hour, four-day workweek so I have more time to garden and canoe race and to spend with my grandkids and stuff," says a Fremont food services manager. Alas, the average workweek increased from 43.6 hours in 1977 to 47.1 hours in 1997. Remember the kids' show *Fraggle Rock*? We're becoming a nation of Doozers.

It helps to just say, "No." I'm not talking about drugs. I'm talking about demands of coworkers, children, whomever puts pressure on you to say, "Yes." You can change "no" to "yes" easily, but "yes" is a stubborn squatter. If necessary, buy time to decide how to say, "No." Don't try to be a hero, leaping to everyone's rescue. You can't please everyone, but you can send yourself to the funny farm trying. If you feel overcommitted and overstressed, just say, "No."

Exercise:
Try this: Place your garbage can on your desk and label it "IN." (Use your judgment on this one.)

Say "No" to yourself, too. Remember Habit #1—how important it is to cheer yourself for every success, no matter how small? Too much self-imposed perfectionist pressure will only burn you out. You are more than just a burnt offering to the gods of productivity. Say "No" to yourself, too, to ease the stress and free the octopus.

⨀ *Vacate* ⨀

Tell them you're busy.

—stage actor Kevin Spacey to the owner
of a ringing cell phone in the audience

The Mexican explains to his Irish guest, "Everything here is Mañana, Mañana, Mañana. Do you have a word like that in Ireland?" The Irishman thinks really hard. "No. No word in Irish conveys such urgency." Wouldn't it be wonderful if we never felt pressed for time and stressed to fill it?

The Doozers need a vacation. By the time you look like your passport photo, you know you're ready to use it.

Sadly, fewer people take vacations these days. A 1968 Gallup poll found that 62 percent of Americans took a vacation of at least a week away from home. A 2000 Gallup poll found that just 42 percent take vacations. Too bad, because researchers in New York studied a group of middle-aged men and found the more vacations they take, the lower their risk of death from heart disease.

Vacations don't need to be long; they simply have to vacate you of the stress, the tension, the workload. Try taking an instant vacation. Visit La-la-land. Take a time-out for yourself each day for 10 to 15 minutes. Let your mind travel...slowly wander...gently float...softly day-dream...completely vacate. Create an oasis for yourself—an imaginary world you can visit to relax. It might be somewhere or it might be nowhere. Meditation comes highly recommended. Or relive in your mind the most peaceful moment you can recall.

My most peaceful moment was when a friend and I slowly—*veeeerry* slowly—let our canoe drift into the reeds. A great blue heron plunged its bill into the water, lifted it high, wiggled its head, and gulped down a fish. It stopped. It watched us for a moment. Then it returned to feeding. This process repeated itself several times as we slowly maneuvered closer. At about three yards, we stopped. We sat and watched. It was only for a few minutes, but who's counting when time stands still?

May you find such a peacefully inspiring moment to return to in your mind when you need an instant vacation. It's part of the recipe for happiness.

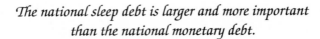 To sleep, perchance to dream

The national sleep debt is larger and more important than the national monetary debt.

—Stanford Sleep Disorders Center director William Dement

Have you ever nodded off while driving? I thought so. Me, too. Half of us do, according to a National Sleep Foundation poll. That's not the best time to visit your La-la-land oasis. A 1999 North Carolina study reveals how a lack of sleep increases the risk of nodding off at the wheel. Hardly surprising, perhaps, but a wake-up call nonetheless.

Detroit Red Wings defenseman Vladimir Konstantinov was placed in a coma when his driver fell asleep and crashed the limo. A sleeping propane truck driver killed himself and injured 23 others near White Plains, News York, even damaging nearby homes with the explosion. A drowsy Alabama student killed himself and injured 21 passengers on a bus he struck. Brakemen and engineers of both trains that collided at Thompsontown, Pennsylvania, in 1988 died because the crew of one of the trains was sleep-deprived. The list of fatigue-induced crashes is almost endless.

Two out of three Americans suffer sleep problems at least a few nights a week. Among the problems are insomnia, snoring, sleep apnea, and restless leg syndrome. (Oooohh, I hate that one.) Not surprisingly, stress is the most frequent sleep disrupter. Stress reduces sleep. Fatigue increases stress. Stress reduces sleep. Fatigue increases stress. Stress and sleeplessness are symbiotic rascals. Together, they make people more grouchy and less happy.

Software consultant Kathleen Coffey explains why she often flies the red-eye home to Charlotte: "Clients aren't going to pay for me to travel half a day." In fact, according to a national poll, almost half of us "sleep less to get more work done."

The growing throngs of red-eye flyers get hit triple hard. First, they cram as much "work" as they can into their day. Then they lose sleep on the flight home. Plus they sacrifice their weekend downtime—their personal time—to stress and fatigue. Not only are they starved for sleep, but they are gripped by a time famine as well.

One out of five Americans admits to fatigue-related errors on the job. In one San Francisco hospital, 42 percent of staff anonymously admitted to causing at least one patient death because of a fatigue-related mistake. The Three Mile Island nuclear accident in Pennsylvania and the Exxon Valdez oil spill off Alaska are just two high-profile disasters attributed in part to sleep-deprivation.

POP QUIZ:

Can you tell when you're going to fall asleep?

ANSWER: Not well enough. Stanford University researchers put 42 young sleep-deprived adults to the test. Every two minutes, a computer prompted them to predict if they would fall asleep in the next two. Half of them were caught off guard by their first sleep. Four out of five times, sleep was predicted, but sleep was also predicted in two out of five non-sleep intervals.

A power nap can restore energy, but as fatigue worsens, rest breaks become less effective. The only antidote for fatigue is full-scale sleep. Sometimes, it even makes sense to sleep on the job. A nap reinvigorates and makes a person more productive. Some companies set up special napping stalls where employees can take official snoozes, like the Kansas City architecture firm with three "spent tents" in the corner of its office.

Unfortunately, people shortchange themselves on sleep. Only a third of Americans sleep the recommended eight hours. Shakespeare's "honey-heavy dew of slumber" is the ultimate luxury in the Age of Overload.

Glued to the TV screen

Most leisure time is filled with activities
that do not make people feel happy or strong.

—psychologists Mihaly Csikszentmihaly and Judith Lefebvre

There's a big chasm between La-la-land and TV land. People who use television as their primary form of entertainment end up less likely to attend a dinner party, visit friends, entertain in their homes, give blood, and send greeting cards. "Chronic television viewing" has even been linked to "giving people the finger." Daytime TV viewing correlates most with civic disengagement. Too much TV cramps your style.

The average American spends three hours a day in front of the television. That's more than exercising, eating, reading, and having sex combined. Together with a sedentary job, television can increase not just stress, but other ailments as well.

Like so many things, television in moderation can be positive. Lucille Peszat, a stress center director, advises that small doses of TV can actually be destressing, especially if it makes you break out laughing. In fact, television is one way we can slow down and relax. So is playing cards or a board game, which offers some social benefits. So are petting an animal and gardening, which put us in touch with nature. So is reading and knitting and ironing and listening to music. If television is balanced equally with a variety of destressers, it can be helpful.

It's not just the quantity of TV that counts, it's the quality. Shows that make you bust a gut (not literally, I hope) help reduce stress. Shows with violence, suspense, or sadness actually increase your stress...even if you love the show. The music, the shouting, the sound effects: they are designed to increase tension. Just after I learned this, Chantal watched a paranormal show while I was reading in the same room. I listened...without watching. The sounds were horrible. They were painful. No wonder they cause stress.

Pennsylvania educator George Gerbner adds that brutality on TV leaves people with "the mean world syndrome," feeling vulnerable in a world full of threats and violence.

Televisions, along with VCRs, video games, and computer screens, serve as a kind of mutant babysitter in many households. Once upon a time, social skills, cultural values, emotional connections were passed down through time children spent playing with friends, siblings, parents, and relatives. Will children raised by robots make the same happiness we can?

Get out of behind that 693-inch screen. Better yet, move out. Stretch your arms. Warm up those legs. It's time for your workout!

∞ **Get exercise** ∞

I never felt happier or more energetic.

—Halifax shoe store manager Jill Hackett after two years
of working out at the gym

Moving your stones is great exercise, and exercise moves your stones. In fact, exercise beats depression at least as well as medication...and research in North Carolina shows that exercise defends better against a depression rebound. Studies show that moderate exercise makes a person feel better about her situation.

Exercise also boosts our immune systems. And of course, it reduces stress.

Most doctors recommend aerobic exercises such as walking, swimming, bicycling, racquet sports, dancing, and skating. A brisk walk also provides a change of scenery and fresh air. It's cheap, convenient, and one size fits all...except for the shoes, of course. When you walk, pick out shoes meant for the purpose. It takes more than 400 steps to walk a mile, each one pounding your full weight into the ground.

For maximum stress relief, I recommend swimming (or any other in-water sport). Swimming gives your whole body a good workout. Water is also an antigravitational device. The buoyancy of the water releases physical tension from your muscles and joints—tension that builds up during the day from the combined forces of stress and gravity. A quick swim before bed can also be the lullaby that seduces the Sandman. Soaking in a bubble bath is relaxing, too, but make sure to also get some exercise.

Exercise:
Come on, I have to give you an exercise in this section. List all the physical activities you enjoy. Now squeeze them into your weekly schedule. Come on, push. Push. Squeeze them in. If you find you're not strong enough to squeeze them into your schedule, you clearly need more exercise.

∞ *Bonus, bonus, bonus, bonus* ∞

Life would be so much easier
if we could just stretch the days out like salt water taffy.

—Olympic gold medal gymnast Mary Lou Retton

Here is a bonus list of some of the best stress-busters. You don't have to choose every one, but most doctors recommend a variety of physical and mental rest, combined with exercise and good nutrition.

- Stand up. Standing boosts blood circulation in your legs, buttocks, and back.
- Stretch. This is the seventh inning stretch, after all. Make funny faces to stretch tense muscles around the corners of your mouth.
- Take a deep breath, expand your abdomen...and focus all your attention on your breathing.
- Big laugh. Humor helps us gain perspective. When you laugh, you take in six times more oxygen, says Tampa humor doctor John Morreall.
- Hug somebody (just somebody who wants a hug, please). Toledo-based Health Care & Retirement trains its employees to hug each other because "the average human needs eight to ten hugs a day."
- Book a massage. Shiatsu, reflexology, and Swedish massage have all been reported to reduce stress.
- New York psychologist Vivien Wolsk says, "Simple household tasks such as ironing or doing laundry can offer drug-free ways of coping with stress."
- Try relaxing music. Music can change your heart rate and reduce your blood pressure.
- Eat healthier: more nutrition, less fat. Ask yourself this: What are the four major food groups? If you answer sugar, caffeine, alcohol, and fat, better return to eating school.
- Cut back on smoking.
- Cut the caffeine. Oakville, Ontario, physician David Posan says, "Seventy-five percent to 80 percent of my patients notice a benefit."
- Drink more water and juice. Drink less alcohol.
- Get a pet. Fish are especially soothing (in a tank, not on your plate!).

PART III
HAPPY WITH OTHERS

HABIT # *8*

*Do not protect yourself by a fence,
but rather by your friends.*

—Czech proverb

Through most of this book, you've been reading about how you make your choices, how you have to live up to your own standards, how you should not allow anyone else to control your happiness. After all, happiness has to come from within.

But wouldn't it be so much easier if you could just get rid of those people who bring you down—**POOF!**, those who make you feel worthless—**POOF!**, the ones who try to tell you how you should act or look or talk or dress or think—**POOF!**? And wouldn't it be wonderful if you could surround yourself by positive, upbeat, gloom-free people who support you, who value you for who you are, who accept your choices, who build you up?

You've heard the old adage that you can judge a person by the company he keeps. It is so true. A person surrounded by positive people sees the world through those elusive rose-colored glasses. A person surrounded by negative people sees very little through mud-stained glasses.

Choose your friends wisely. Surround yourself with YouBet people. What's a YouBet? That's what we'll learn in Chapter 16.

CHAPTER 16

The company you keep

Hold a true friend with both your hands.

—Nigerian proverb

Friends come. Friends go. And some stick around. It's something that just seems to happen, but maybe it's something worth thinking about. What kind of friends do you have? What kind of company do you keep? Do you have friends you should dump? Have you lost touch with friends you should hold close?

People come in all types: extroverts and introverts, physical and sedentary, intellectual and practical, emotional and aloof, positive and negative. Most of us are a combination of all these characteristics and so many more. But some traits grab our attention more than others.

Exercise:

On a sheet of paper, list all the people you call friends, including brothers, sisters, cousins, and buddies you spend time with. Beside each name, write three words that best describe that person's character or personality.

∞ *People are contagious* ∞

*Negative people are really the only barriers to happiness,
because negativity spreads like weeds.*

—New York entrepreneur Marcia Kilgore

Habit #8 is to choose YouBet people. These are the kind of people who light up the room with energy when they enter. You probably know somebody like this. When he or she lights up the room, what really happens? Do the walls glow? Does the table levitate? Do the chairs come to life? No, it's the people that glow. It's their spirit that levitates. It's their mood that comes to life.

Happiness is contagious. Isn't that wonderful news? You catch it just by being around positive, upbeat, happy people. Happiness loves company.

Misery loves company, too. "Bad moods can be as contagious as viruses," warns Hawaii psychology professor Elaine Hatfield. Pessimism percolates, and its aroma invades our consciousness. If we listen to enough negative, pessimistic, unhappy, critical comments, it's easy to start thinking that way, too.

Happiness. Misery. They're both contagious. And everybody is a carrier, everyone is a pollinator. Some people carry more happiness, some more misery. If you have to become intimate with a happiness carrier or a misery carrier, which would you choose? Which *will* you choose? Happiness is a choice, you see?

Exercise:

Let's look at that list of your friends you made earlier. You might have written "happy" or "joyful" or "outgoing" or "enthusiastic" or "generous" beside some names. These are YouBet people. Beside others, you might have written "complaining" or "negative" or "miserable" or "sad" or "boring." These are YeahBut people. Others might not be very much of either. Determine which people are YouBets, which ones are YeahButs, and which ones fall somewhere in between.

◎ *YeahButs and YouBets* ◎

Every newspaper has a special department, called the Bummer Desk,
which is responsible for digging up depressing front-page stories like
DOORBELL USE LINKED TO LEUKEMIA and OZONE LAYER
COMPLETELY GONE DIRECTLY OVER YOUR HOUSE.

—humorist Dave Barry

Your happiness depends in part on the company you keep. If you surround yourself with YeahBut people, woe is you. YeahBut people are the pessimists who can always find a cloud for every silver lining and see only rain when they look at a rainbow. Whine, whine, whine. Complain, complain, complain.

You're planning a career change? You're preparing your resume? You're ready to roll? Not to worry. The YeahBut people will slam on the brakes. "Yeah, but can you really do it?" "Yeah, but the job market is tight." "Yeah, but what about security?"

Thinking of marrying that special someone you've been dating? YeahButs can help you escape your foolishness. "Yeah, but he might not treat you right." "Yeah, but what if she's not the right one." "Yeah, but what if there's someone better?"

YeahButs are the gremlins that fuel inertia. From them, silence truly is golden.

Other people might help you overcome the destructive YeahBut influence. They are the YouBet people—the optimists who can always find a silver lining under every cloud and a pot of gold at the end of every rainbow.

About that career change, what do YouBets think? "You bet you can do it." "You bet you've got what it takes." About those wedding bells you're hearing, "You bet it's right." "You bet you can make it work." "You bet he'll be a great husband." YouBets find the world champion in you. They are the kind of people who give you the bolsterism we saw in Chapter 9.

YouBet and YeahBut people are contagious. YouBets are yaysayers. They lift your spirits with them up into the clouds. They are the spark plugs of your life. YeahButs are naysayers. They drag you with them through the swine trough. They are both contagious, so you want to be very careful about the company you keep.

POP QUIZ:
What does the "nt" stand for in "don't"?
ANSWER: Negative thinking. When you take negative thinking away from "don't," you have "do," a positive. Here's the math:

Don't (negative)
- nt (negative thinking)
= do (positive)

You might have heard that people who say, "It can't be done" should not interrupt those who are doing it. So how do you remove negative thinking from your social circle? The secret lies in the Wheel of Friendship.

The Wheel of Friendship

Given the trend toward smaller families, tentative marriages, unstable jobs, and community breakdown, we need our friends now more than ever.

—Boston writer Linda Matchan

Wheel of Friendship is not a game show. There are no consonants to guess, no vowels to buy. But the Wheel of Friendship is the game of life. Our friend, Margaret, first introduced us to the idea. The Wheel is like a map of everybody we know.

In the hub of the wheel are the really, really, really close friendships we've nurtured. These are the people we rely on emotionally, the people we feel are closest, the people with whom we share the most.

Around the rim are the masses of peek-a-boo people who enter, leave, or stay in our lives. They are people with whom we interact, but we really don't care whether we know them or not. You probably know hundreds of such people at work, in the neighborhood, at stores you frequent, in classes you attend. Occasionally, one of them starts working his way up the spokes. That's what making friends is all about.

On the spokes, between the hub and the rims, are all the people we might call "friends," but many of them might, in fact, be better called "acquaintances." These are people we enjoy knowing, some very much. We share some of ourselves with them, but not usually our deepest feelings, and we wouldn't really want to be around them all the time. The more we value them—the closer we are to them—the more they approach the hub. The less they mean to us, the closer they are to the rim. Of course, we grow closer to some people over time and further from others, so nobody's position on the Wheel of Friendship is fixed.

There are a few things you should know about the Wheel. As it turns, the rims spin faster than the hub. In fact, the closer to the rim, the more likely an acquaintance is to fly off when the wheel hits a bump in the road. These people are more likely to be the ones you leave behind. The friends in the hub are the most secure, even when the road is bumpier than a camel's back.

You might also notice that the hub is small. There aren't very many people who can fit in the hub. Margaret told us a person is lucky if she can count more than three or four people in the hub and more than a couple handfuls nearby on the spokes. Even if they drift away, they're somehow still there.

By the way, parents don't count. Most people have psychologically different relationships with their parents. But brothers and sisters count, as do spouses, and some people are lucky enough to count them among their very close friends. But whoever is in your hub, may it be somebody. We all need intimacy.

Exercise:

Draw your own Wheel of Friendship. Make it large enough to write names on it. Now write in all the names from the list you were working on. Place those people you consider extremely close in the hub, regardless of what adjectives you use to describe them. On the spokes, place people closer to the hub if you consider them closer friends and farther if you consider them less close. What you are doing now is placing them where you think they have been recently, not where you think they should be.

∽ *The happy lollipop* ∽

Did you know that if you hug someone long enough you can feel the heat from her body for some time after you let go?

—*Philadelphia Inquirer* columnist Lucia Herndon

When a rat pup is born, its mother licks and grooms it. Some pups get very little attention; others are licked until you'd think their skin would peel off. These lollipop pups grow up to be less fearful, more resistant to stress, and more curious. They are happier with life.

People are a lot like rats (in a good way). Those with a close friendship, someone they consider to be a soul mate, are happier. They know it, too. Sometimes we are lucky enough to marry a soul mate. Sometimes, our spouses cling to the spokes of the wheel. I'm lucky to have my wife right in the hub of my Wheel.

Generally, married type people tend to be happier than unmarried type people. A marriage or similar relationship provides an opportunity for more intimacy, more sharing, more true human contact than other relationships usually offer.

On my wedding day, I toasted my wife Chantal, with an ode to her many qualities. "But it's your *joie de vivre* I love the most," I concluded. We had met on the telephone, through one of those telephone dating lines, and we instantly felt the attraction. There was excitement in both our voices. We both had so much joy, such a zest for life. We had so much to give each other.

After several hours of vibrant discussions on the telephone came the moment of truth. We would meet face to face. But would the chemistry be there? I admit I was terrified. What if the magic so obvious on the telephone just wasn't there in real life?

Thank God Chantal's joy is as contagious in person as on the telephone. I am a lucky man. For many people, it's not as easy to place their partners in their hubs. So many people are not that close to the person they commit to. I believe that is one of the true tragedies of life (a hint for people still searching for a partner).

Some psychologists believe that social support, or companionship, is the most important factor contributing to happiness. Nobody is self-sufficient. Even Saudi Arabia, land of sand-dune camel caravans, has to import both camels and sand.

A study of 7,000 Alameda County adults shows that people with the strongest social ties, whether with family, friends, or community, are at least two times less likely to die from any cause than those with more isolated lives. This is just one of many studies that show how important social support is, not just to our emotional well-being, but also to our physical well-being. In fact, it is becoming more and more clear that what's good for happiness is good for our bodies.

One study shows that during the 1980s, the ability of children and teenagers to manage their own emotions and their relationships declined. Forty-two measures of self-management and social skills decreased. None increased. Renowned psychologist and *Emotional Intelligence* author Daniel Goleman attributes this disturbing trend to two-income families in which children spend little time with their parents, and to television, which replaces the social contact children once experienced.

In Chapter 13, we learned about how fear of speaking, of socializing, of talking to strangers can rob us of happiness. Here's another reason to talk to strangers: even just increasing social interaction has been shown to increase happiness. If you work at home or are a stay-at-home parent, you know exactly what I mean. I work from home, but at least my job requires me to speak frequently on the phone, attend meetings, and meet with people over lunch.

A colleague of mine told me about a restaurant he frequents. The owner hires only seniors from a group home as waiters. My colleague told me they are the friendliest waiters he ever met, because they are so thrilled just to get out and meet people.

Nonetheless, most social interactions are not very intimate, even when they are satisfying. When we invite guests over for dinner, we don't expect them to mention that the potatoes were over-cooked. We expect them to be selectively candid. And you might prefer they don't talk about their anxieties, health problems, or the fight they had last night (not even the fun they might have had last night!).

The more intimate the relationship, the more likely people are to offer candid and intimate details...and the more likely you are to welcome those details. We need casual interactions, but we also need intimacy. The Council of Economic Advisers reports that teenagers who dine with their families are less likely to mix it up with drugs, alcohol, violence, and sex. But, oops, Minnesota psychologist William Doherty reports that half of U.S. families watch television during dinner. That should worry anyone concerned about our collective well-being and the future of the family...and give us yet another reason to reconsider how we use television (see Chapter 15). We have to foster situations that lead to intimacy.

∞ **Who's in your hub?** ∞

Laugh, and the world laughs with you, weep, and you weep alone.

—poet Ella Wilcox

Returning to our Wheel of Friendship, what happens if we include negative friends—YeahBut people—in the hub? Let's suppose we include people who won't comfort us when we're down, who won't cheer us when we succeed, who won't encourage us to fulfil our dreams. Let's suppose we surround ourselves with people who complain and whine. That's not a very sound hub for a wheel. That's not the intimacy we need. That's the wrong virus to catch.

When someone is aggressively negative, they are bound to lose all their friends. One survey respondent explained, "I don't have a single good friend left. Do you know why? Because I told them all exactly what I think of them."

When people are more passively negative (complaining, depressing, boring), they might sometimes fool us. You've probably noticed that some YeahBut people are also cling-ons. Like burrs from a bush, they cling to you. You try to shake them off, but they wrap themselves around you all the harder. They want into your hub. Don't let them.

The people you let into your hub wield the greatest influence on how you feel, how you think, who you are. They help you paint your portrait. They have the power to help you move stones to your Stairway, or they can actually compel you to move stones back to the Wall. The Bible might say that the lamb will lie down with the lion, but experience tells the lamb to beware the lion bearing a mint jelly gift. People need intimacy. That means sharing, caring, and licking wounds, not holding them open.

Sometimes you might also be tempted to associate with someone because she is rich, powerful, popular—because she wears the Mask of Success. If she's an upbeat, positive person, why not befriend her? But if she's a negative YeahBut person…Gotcha! The Merchants of Misery strike again. Let them peddle Ms. Negative's friendship to somebody else.

Ol' Dumpy Humpy was enjoying life perched upon his wall. (It seems he scaled the Great Wall of Misery.) He could see clear across the garden and watch the birds in flight. The flowers were his friends.

One day, a mushroom sprang forth. "Oh dear," the mushroom complained. "It's so damp here." (Of course, mushrooms grow only where it's damp.) Dumpy Humpy listened.

"Goodness, but it's cold today," the mushroom whined. Dumpy Humpy sympathized.

"Yeach! I'm up to my stem in dirt!" The Mushroom cried. Dumpy Humpy felt sad for the poor mushroom.

"Why am I all alone?" wailed the mushroom. "I wish I'd never been born." Dumpy Humpy took pity and bent over to tell the lonely mushroom that it's also lonely at the top, when whoa-oa-oa… aaaaaaiiiaaaii…**CRASH!** And that was the end of Dumpy Humpy. YeahBut people can bring an otherwise happy person crashing to the ground just like poor ol' Dumpy Humpy.

A strong wheel has a strong hub. You want friends who help lift you from misery, cheer your successes, encourage you to be your best. You want people who bolster your mood, your resolve, your spirit. You want YouBet people who can help you build your Stairway to Heaven. Habit #8 is to seek out those positive, uplifting YouBet people, to fill your hub with Yayists.

Our friend, Nathalie, has a poster on her wall: "Friends are the flowers in the garden of life." What kind of plants do you want growing in the garden of your life? Rose bushes? Tiger lilies? Or milkweeds and thistles?

POP QUIZ:

If one synchronized swimmer drowns, is the other one obliged to drown, too?

ANSWER: Thankfully, we don't know yet.

If a friend of yours drowns herself in pessimism, negative talk, and misery, you are not legally required to drown with her. Be supportive, try to help. She might be a genuine friend, supportive and caring, going through a hard time. She might need you to be her YouBet friend. She might need the bolsterism you learned in Chapter 9. Don't forget that most people are some combination of YouBets and YeahButs.

But if, over the long run, she's determined to be miserable...oh well. Push her further out along the spokes if she drags you down. Why should both of you drown in misery when one of you wants to be happy?

∽ *Rebuild your wheel* ∽

Wiggle free from hugs that cut off your circulation.

—horoscope in *The Village Voice*

Texas researchers asked independent observers to judge the quality of various social interactions. Unbeknownst to them, the subjects had been chosen for their high levels of either positive affect (feeling good about life) or negative affect (feeling bad about life). The observers judged the interactions between the positive people to be of a higher quality. I'm sure you'll find interactions with positive people more satisfying, too.

Habit #8 was the inspiration for the Rotary movement. In 1905, Paul Harris wanted to build in the big city the same kind of congeniality he felt in the villages where he grew up. Today, city dwellers still seek that sense of community the Rotary movement sought to preserve. Build a warm, friendly community in the hub of your Wheel of Friendship. Cast the YeahBut people out.

Exercise:

1. Look at your Wheel of Friendship. Compare the names on the wheel to those on your list. Are there some in the hub or close to the hub who would bring Dumpy Humpy crashing down? For each YeahBut person, decide how far out to place the name, and decide to stop socializing with the person unless absolutely necessary. This can be scary if several of your close friends are YeahBut people. You might fear losing most of your friends.

2. So ask yourself if there are some names far out on the spokes who carry uplifting positive viruses of happiness? For each YouBet person, decide how close to the hub you want him to be, and decide to start socializing with him more. Start by calling to share good news, to suggest an activity together. As you start to know them better, call them also when you need support. Tell them, "I always feel so good around you. I'm feeling a little sad right now, and I believe that talking with you will cheer me up." Then, let them cheer you up, and thank them for making you feel so much better. If you don't let them cheer you up, if you don't let the virus of happiness infect you, they might see in you a YeahBut person and back away.

3. Don't forget to give people the opportunity to move closer along the spokes if their outlook improves (for example, if they are inspired by this book to make their lives happier). YeahButs can become YouBets.

Sarah Sheep cries, "Watch out for that falling stone." Bray Goat shouts, "C'mon Sarah, you can do it! We're almost there." And sure enough, Sarah Sheep and Bray Goat have almost reached the top. They are almost out of the well. How did they make it? Battered and bruised, sore and tired, somehow they found the energy and the strength.

The secret is that the sheep and the goat are YouBet people. Well, YouBet *animals*. They support each other, they try to be positive for one another, and despite a few moments of weakness, they complain very little. Bray Goat thinks, "Am I ever lucky Sarah's on my side." Sarah thinks, "He may be a silly old goat, but at least he supports me. That's the kind of friend I need."

When all else fails, try reciting the senility prayer: "God, grant me the senility to forget the people I never liked anyway, the good fortune to run into those I do, and the eyesight to tell the difference." Any resemblance to the serenity prayer in Chapter 1 is, of course, purely coincidental.

HABIT # *9*

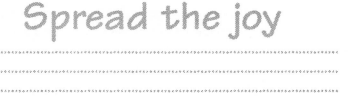

Spread the joy

Those who wish to sing always find a song.

—Swedish proverb

There are some things that taste best when shared. Love is one of those things. I can love you. You can love me. But both of us would enjoy our love a lot better if we love each other. Ideas are also most useful when shared. If two people each share an idea with the other, each one has two ideas.

What's in a name?

My brother's godmother is Joy. When she spreads the *Joy*, she does it quite literally, sharing herself with those around New York City and the world needing her help.

Joy is like love and ideas. The more we share it, the more we have. By now, we've learned a lot about getting joy. We've learned how to value what we do, who we are, and what we have. We've learned to look ahead to the future and to overcome our fears. We've beaten stress and surrounded ourselves with positive people. We bring so much joy just waiting to be shared.

Joy is like manure. No, really. You can grow great crops one year, but if you don't spread the manure around, sooner or later the ground loses its ability to grow strong crops. Spread your joy around, fertilize your friendships, your environment, your world. Spread that joy as thick as you can. We'll be looking at two ways to spread the joy. In Chapter 17, we'll look at how we relate to people around us.

Legal secretary Joan Binetti is often asked, "How can you always be so happy?" This seemed strange to me. "I think they're asking the wrong question," I told her. "They should be asking 'How can I become as happy as you are?'" As motivational speaker Peter Legge points out, why tell someone, "Have a great day," when we really mean, "Make it a great day." That's how to spread the joy to people we know.

POP QUIZ:
Why is Mona Lisa smiling?
ANSWER: She was spreading the joy to Leonardo da Vinci (and to millions of secret admirers).

We'll also be looking, in Chapter 18, at how to spread the joy beyond our own little world to those who most need a booster shot of the stuff.

A fine example is the North Carolina mother who gave up a portion of her liver to save the life of a six-month-old boy whose parents she hardly knew.

So make it a great day...and a great world!

CHAPTER 17

Put on a happy face

Fortune will call at the smiling gate.

—Japanese proverb

Everywhere I go, I see the Happy Face—that bright yellow sun with big black eyes and a big black smile. You might even remember that song from way, way back: "Spread sunshine all over the place, just put on a happy face."

It seems to me the world is divided into two camps: Pro-face and anti-face. The pro-face crowd loves to see the happy, yellow face. It brings joy. It uplifts their spirits. The anti-face crowd scowls at the very sight of it. They are convinced the happier-than-life face is a secret plot meant to undermine their right to scowl by coercing everyone to wear a smile, even when they don't feel like it. Or, maybe they're just jealous. I'm pro-face.

Everybody has the right to scowl. I'm sure I read that somewhere in the Bible or the Constitution…or was it on the bathroom wall? Okay, so it's our right to scowl, but does that mean we should? While we should-n't wander around in a sedative-induced daze, grinning just to prove we can, there is something to be said for smiling. And I'm about to say it.

∞ **Sit up and smile** ∞

Why I had to explain why I smiled all the time is beyond me.

—Prince Edward Island golfer Lorie Kane

Charlemagne, king of the Franks, sat smiling for 401 years. His funeral directors could not bear to bury him, so they embalmed him and propped him up on his throne with a smile on his face from 814 to 1215. You, too, can prop yourself up with a smile. In fact, research shows that you can actually prop up your emotions with facial expressions. So you want to be happy? Smile. It works.

POP QUIZ:
How funny are cartoons?
ANSWER: More so when people exercise the same facial muscles they use to smile. Less so when they frown. On the other hand, positive scenes elicit less pleasure when people suppress muscles used in smiling. Smiling really can make you feel happier.

Like a ventriloquist, giving voice to your emotions makes them come alive. We discussed this in Chapter 10. Venting your frustrations doesn't release your anger; it captures more of it. Expressing emotions verbally or facially makes us feel the emotions all the more. So smiling makes us feel happier. How does this work? Is it magic? No, it's neurology. When we move our facial muscles, we change the blood flow to and from various sections of the brain. That's why, when we smile, we feel the emotion that smiling demonstrates: happiness. So smiling to simulate happiness can bring us the very happiness we're faking.

Happiness researcher David Myers says we should all tell ourselves little white lies: "Do we wish to change ourselves in some important way?...Well, a potent strategy is to get up and start doing that very thing.

Don't worry that you don't feel like it. Fake it. Pretend self-esteem. Feign optimism. Simulate outgoingness." Self-improvement guru Dale Carnegie gives similar advice: "Act as if you are already happy and that will tend to make you happy." In other words, if you fake it, you'll make it.

By the way, it appears this works on others, as well. Researchers have found that if you idealize your partner, he will eventually share your idealized image of himself. In other words, you can create the relationship you want as the romance progresses. This makes sense when you think of the reverse—an abusive spouse who constantly tells his partner she is worthless makes her end up feeling worthless. So it stands to reason that an adoring spouse who tells his partner she is an angel builds up her self-esteem. If you really want to destroy your partner's life, you can easily find enough about her to crush her. But if you really want to share your joy with your partner, you can easily find enough about her to fill her heart with joy.

Remember the positive illusions we learned about in Chapter 5? This is just another way to put them to use. Some things can be faked. You can make yourself feel happier just by smiling. The joker-face clown feels happiness easier than the poker-face gambler. But there are a few catches.

Smiling with your mouth alone is unlikely to make you feel truly happy. Researchers report that the "Duchenne smile" (named after French neurologist Guillaume Duchenne) is a better sign of true joy. The Duchenne smile uses muscles around the eyes as well as the mouth. When I discovered this, I finally understood why I've always been attracted to women whose whole faces light up when they smile, not just their mouths. Now I'm married to just such a woman, and I benefit from full-face smiles every day.

You've got to really mean it. You've got to really want to be happy. Simply forcing a fake or sarcastic smile you don't mean will not on its own make you feel happy. However, the best way to make yourself feel better when you feel like frowning is to grin from ear to ear—if you really want to feel better, that is.

You might also have heard it takes more muscles to frown than to smile. No wonder smiling makes us happier! This certainly makes poor old Bray Goat feel better. As tired as he is from shaking off stones and stepping up, he knows that all he has to do is smile to feel happy. Okay, not quite happy, but it does bolster his strength and make him feel a little better.

As a bonus, chain-smilers don't worry about dropping their smiles. When we crack a glass, it breaks. When we crack a smile, it strengthens. So don't be afraid to crack a smile.

As much as a smile can make you feel happier, your posture can affect your emotions, too. An upright posture increases confidence and positive feelings. A slouched posture increases negative feelings.

Happy people also tend to take bigger steps. This rings true for me. I find that a brisk walk lifts my mood—I actually feel full of positive energy after going for a brisk walk. Try it; you might find it helps you, too.

So, here's the recipe: smile, stand up straight, walk fast, and, oh yes, nod. (Go ahead and nod right now.) Nodding makes people feel more positive, as one experiment reveals. Shaking your head from side to side has the opposite effect.

I haven't seen any studies about this next one, but I'll go out on a limb and say that clapping probably will make you feel great, too. Try it. Applaud yourself right now. Applaud somebody else, too.

POP QUIZ: ....
So did Charlemagne's upright posture and posthumous smile make him feel happier propped up on his throne?
ANSWER: No, he was dead, and dead people usually don't feel much of anything. You're not dead, so straighten up and smile.

∞ *Ha ha ha ha ha ha ha!* ∞

The motto in our family is: crack jokes, not heads.

—New York humorist Angela Barbeisch

That's the sound of my mother-in-law laughing. Ha ha ha ha ha ha ha! It's one of those contagious laughs that resonates around the room and makes everyone feel good. Most of all, it makes her feel good.

It's important to be able to laugh at ourselves, too. Wonder what the funniest book ever would look like? Open it up, and there's a mirror inside. When we laugh at ourselves, we take things a little less seriously—and we take ourselves much less seriously. How does this make us happier? It helps us let go of anger, forgive ourselves for mistakes, and fear less what others might think of us.

When you can't laugh at yourself, laugh at whatever else you can find. I remember Chantal accusing me of eating all the cookies. I insisted that was not so: "I ate only those that were left." It seemed like hours before we stopped laughing.

Laughter is good exercise for your heart and your lungs, but most of all for your soul. You inhale six times more oxygen when you laugh than when you talk. Laughter releases endorphins in your brain. Endorphins hate the color blue, so if that's how you're feeling, laughter will help make things look a little rosier before long. Apparently, laughter also activates T lymphocytes (which are not dinosaurs) and gamma interferon (which are not new *Star Trek* characters). San Diego psychologist Harold Greenwald says, "Laughter and depression are genuinely incompatible."

Just as smiling can make both you and your partner happier, so can laughter. Is it any wonder that women are attracted to a man with a sense of humour? So go ahead and crack a joke and a smile.

∞ *Extrovert thyself* ∞

May you live all the days of your life.

—English satirist Jonathan Swift

The extrovert enjoys the company of people. The extrovert welcomes people and talks to them. The extrovert smiles at people and speaks to them. So how do people react? They speak back. They smile back. They respond. With everybody speaking and smiling back at the extrovert, it's easy for her to make friends.

And the science shows that extroverts are happier. In Chapter 13 we defied glossophobia, and one of our exercises helped us develop a plan for entering a room of strangers. By overcoming shyness, even an introvert can feign extroversion…and what happens when we fake it? That's right, we make it. This won't necessarily make an extrovert out of an introvert (which is good, because introverts also have great qualities), but it will help introverts benefit from the happy habits of extroverts.

The science also tells us that people who like themselves tend to be extroverts. So if we rewind even further, *vvvvvhhhrrrrhhmmm*, we find ourselves in Chapter 7 shining like a diamond. Having learned to like ourselves, we can assume that other people will like us, too. And that's a self-fulfilling attitude. When we assume people like us, the world is a much safer place, and there's much less reason to feel shy.

Extroverts are more likely to get married, find fulfilling jobs, make new friends, and improve their lives. And all that with a smile around the mouth and a few friendly words inside. If you are shy, it's worth planning a way to crawl out of your shell, smile, and talk with more people. It's fine to be an introvert, but why not also benefit from the same actions as extroverts.

Others will want to help you

The only way to have a friend is to be one.

—cleric Ralph Waldo Emerson

Your smile is your calling card. It's the first thing someone sees when he meets you. It creates that first impression on which you will be judged. And it determines how that other person will treat you. A warm, inviting smile is like a welcome mat to other people.

I had a firsthand lesson in the value of spreading smiles. I was running a friend's political campaign, one of eight contested races in the city. The campaign was just over a month long, but it didn't take long for campaign workers across the city to hear about the Beardsley campaign, where people had fun, where everyone's contributions were valued, where people were made to feel happy and worthwhile. We practiced bolsterism. By the end of the campaign, our volunteers had doubled in number—at the expense of some of the other campaigns whose stressed-out leaders micro-managed their teams.

Even a child's temperament determines how people react to him. How people react, in turn, determines how the child's temperament develops. Although temperament is more permanent in adults, the action-reaction equation remains. How you act determines how others react to you. If you smile, others feel good about you and treat you well. That gives you a reason to smile. On the other hand, if you frown, others feel uncomfortable about you and treat you poorly. And that could make you frown even more.

The company plant had just expanded, and it was the first day on the job for the new workers. One of them asked the foreman, "What are the people like in this plant?" The foreman didn't answer. Instead, he asked the worker, "Where you worked last, what were the people like?"

"They smiled a lot," replied the stranger. "They were friendly people, always willing to lend a hand."

"Then you'll enjoy this job, for you'll find your coworkers here are the same," the foreman assured him.

A few minutes later, another new employee approached the foreman about the type of coworkers he would have. "What about where you come from?" asked the foreman. "What are the people like in that plant?"

"Bunch of grumpies, always scowling and muttering," complained the new employee.

"Dear me, I'm afraid you'll find the same type of people here," the foreman responded.

People treat us as we treat them. How we see others is a function of how they see us. It's simple human nature.

Help others to help you smile

Nothing is so contagious as enthusiasm;
it moves stones, it charms brutes.

—British novelist Edward Bulwer-Lytton

If you want to benefit from others' contagious joy, you have to do your part, too. You can help others smile around you. Studies show that one person's interpersonal action tends to invite a complementary response from the other person (friendliness invokes friendliness, dominance evokes submission, etc.). Every face you meet is a mirror. Shine a smile on someone else's face, and see how your smile reflects back at you. Bask in the glow of your own smile reflected in the joy you bring to others.

You might have heard about Mike and Pete, two boys who were told to clean the stables. Mike took one look at the straw and the manure and said, "Whew, this is the worst." Pete grabbed a shovel and started working. He even began whistling. Mike asked, "What on earth have you got to be so happy about?"

Pete answered, "With all this manure, there's got to be a pony in here somewhere. Mike thought about it for a moment. He picked up his shovel...and he began to whistle.

Exercise:
Try smiling at everyone you meet, even people you pass in
the street. See how much better you—and they—feel.

When I was working in Planet Cubicle, I got hourly doses of joy bounding over the divider from the next "office." That was Rosalinda of the contagious laughter, with plenty of it to share. These days, I get that from my mother-in-law. There's just something about a no-holds-barred laughter that lifts your spirits.

The importance of presenting yourself in a positive light is best illustrated by an experiment that put physicians to the test. Two groups of doctors were given the same statistics. One group was told that 10 of every 100 patients would die in surgery. The other group was informed that 90 percent would live. Although these are identical statistics, and doctors are educated and intelligent, the two groups reacted differently. Twice as many doctors given the positive spin chose surgery compared to those who heard the negative spin.

One of the best ways to share the joy is to tell others about these habits. They worked for me, they're starting to work for you...why not share them with people you care about? Or even better, share them with someone who's been acting grumpy to you!

Smiles are contagious. Laughter is, too. And enthusiasm is most contagious of all. If you love life, if you thrill to be alive, if everything is an exciting challenge, people around you will fill with enthusiasm. Be a bright, bold color, not a dull gray. After all, who ever felt excited about gray?

The best part of smiling and laughing and enthusing is not that it makes you feel great. It's not that it makes the other person feel great. It's that if you make the other person happy, joyful, and enthusiastic, you'll catch her great mood—that same mood that your joy and enthusiasm gave her. See how easy it is to enlist others in your climb up your Stairway to Heaven? And isn't it exciting to help someone else up her Stairway at the same time?

So do yourself a favor and put on a happy face—not just on yourself, but on everyone around you.

CHAPTER 18

Real virtuality

A little help is better than a lot of pity.

—Celtic proverb

Some people accuse the happiness movement of being selfish, hedonistic, self-absorbed. They rightly suggest that we should not live just to please ourselves. But the fact is that people are less self-absorbed when they are happy. Instead of bemoaning their misery, they share their joy. Happiness makes us more altruistic.

In one experiment, researchers passed by a telephone booth and "accidentally" dropped some papers. In some cases, the researchers had left money to be unexpectedly found by telephone users. Those whose moods were brightened by the unexpected find were more likely to help pick up the papers. Just feeling upbeat made people more giving.

Studies show that happy people are more cooperative with others. Studies also show that tolerance of minorities is one of the results of increasing happiness. Social scientists find happy people more likely to participate in the political process and more prone to social contact.

The reverse is true. When we are miserable, we don't please others. Studies show that unhappy people are more self-focused and socially withdrawn. The link between happiness and holiness has a long history. The Dalai Lama talks about the importance of being happy. Almost every religion gives us reason to rejoice, to dance, to be happy—and at the same time to give, to share, to care. Let's face it, Ebenezer Scrooge and the Grinch were not world-class philanthropists ...until they got happy.

Yes, happy people tend to be giving people. With six billion people in the world, imagine the good we could do if we were six billion *happy* people.

∞ *The riddle of altruism* ∞

The more I did for others, the less I thought about me,
and the better I felt about myself.

—recovering brain tumor patient Brian Asenjo

If happy people are generous, then generous people are happy. Altruism makes us happier by giving us meaning and by taking our attention off our own problems and onto the well-being of others.

Some philosophers suggest there is no such thing as altruism. When we help somebody, we do it to make ourselves happier, to feel fulfilled, to be loved, to feel worthwhile—whatever the reason, it is for our own good that we help others. If we don't please others, we'll be miserable.

If you're familiar with the dour 17th century philosopher Thomas Hobbes, who insisted that human kindness did not exist, you would be surprised to hear that he gave money to beggars. When confronted with this, he explained, "I'm just doing this to relieve my own distress at seeing the man's poverty." Actress Susan Sarandon, explaining why she wants to improve society, echoes this sentiment, "I have to explain to my kids why Americans live in boxes on the streets near our home."

POP QUIZ: . . . .
What should be a sales representative's goal?
ANSWER: According to sales trainers, a sales person who
focuses on maximizing commissions is rarely happy. A sales
person who focuses on the customers' needs is likely to feel
fulfilled. But you already knew that from Chapter 2, right?

This notion of the link between happiness and altruism smashes the
traditional notion of the do-good martyr. Do you really have to be miserable to do good? You might have heard the story of the desperate man
who cries out to God, "Lord, the world is in misery. Why don't you do
something?"

God responds, "I did, my son. I sent you."

FRESH-BAKED COOKIES FOR THE HOMELESS

While some pray for God to "do something," others are busy doing
just that. Was Florence Nightingale miserable? Was Saint Francis of
Assisi miserable? Was Mother Teresa miserable? No. They each took

comfort, found joy, felt worthwhile for their deeds. They were exceedingly happy people. Unshackled from desiring comforts, unburdened from pursuing money, relieved of their personal problems, they were free to help others. And their gifts to others filled their lives with meaning, with comfort, with happiness.

In the introduction, I promised to explain why I would share with you this precious information: the nine habits of maximum happiness. By now, you might have guessed. Because doing good makes me feel good. Because it is in spreading joy that I feel joy. It's the same reason my baby brother—the teacher—chose to teach special needs children with learning disabilities and psychological barriers. Truly, it is in giving that we receive.

- Dr. Eric Whitaker founded Project Brotherhood in Woodlawn (Chicago). The project caters to fellow black men, whom he saw falling through the holes in the safety net. From haircuts to job cuts, from broken bones to broken families, his project lends a hand. Why?
- When an 81-year-old lady can't get a booth at a New York City diner, two young men in a booth invite her to join them at their table. Why?
- Entering a museum parking lot, my friend, Nick, holds up a humongous bag of fresh-picked peas for the parking attendant. "Go ahead, take some," he urges. She hesitates, then reaches in and pulls out a handful. "Take some more," he urges again. Why?
- Over time, Carl and Ingrid Schulz, of Wisconsin, took in 98 teenagers in need of a home. Ingrid explains, "We had an extra bed, and that's all you really needed. He (Carl) never questioned where his paycheck went." Why?
- Illinois teenager Bailey Elliott enjoys collecting four-leaf clovers (over 13,000 to date) just to give them away to people who are down on their luck. Why?

- A Virginia judge hands $250 to a newlywed deaf couple being sued for falling short on their rent. Why?

Because it feels good to do good. If the road to Hell is paved with good intentions, the Stairway to Heaven is built from good deeds come true.

Exercise:
List the things in the world that you feel need changing the most. List the people in your community you think need help the most. List the things you read about in the newspaper or watch on the news that make you shake your head in disbelief, frustration, or compassion. Decide which ones you would like to help change. Start phoning around or searching on the Internet for others involved in the same causes and ask, "How can I help?"

'Tis noble to be happy

You make a living by what you get,
but you make a life by what you give.

—Colorado attorney Lane Earnest

Some people insist there is a moral imperative to be happy. I owe it to my wife to be as happy as I possibly can be. She should not have to cope with a moping, miserable grouch. She should be able to wake up to a smiling, affectionate, pleasant husband. That makes her happier. And she owes me the same.

This doesn't mean that we should never be allowed to feel down, nor that moments of melancholy should wrap us up in the guilt quilt. It simply means that we should try to live happy lives for our own sake and for the sake of those we are close to. We owe it to them to be YouBet people.

Happiness is noble. Otherwise, why wish it on someone we love? Have a great day. Happy birthday. Have fun. We want people we care about to enjoy themselves. And if happiness is indeed noble, why would we not pursue it for ourselves, too?

What about our neighbors? Surely if charity begins at home, its next stop should be next door.

POP QUIZ:
How well do you know your neighbors?
ANSWER: Here's what the statistics show:
- Nearly half of us (45 percent) have never spent an evening with one of our next door neighbors.
- Even fewer of us (42 percent) have borrowed that proverbial cup of sugar.
- A quarter of us has never set foot inside a neighbor's home.
- And 15 percent of us don't even know the names of the next door neighbors.

So much for a sense of community. So much for spreading joy far and near...far, maybe, but certainly not near. We are starting to notice effects of estranging ourselves from people around us. Nearly three-quarters of Americans are not satisfied with the state of morality today. That doesn't sound too happy.

Here's a statement that I hope will guide Chantal and me in the right direction. We got his-and-hers matching mugs one Valentines Day. Each has a picture of a child with this inscription: "A hundred years from now it will not matter what my bank account was, the sort of house I lived in, or the kind of car I drove... But the world may be different because I was important in the life of a child." We want to share our creativity, our intelligence, our interests with our children. But most of all, we want to share our joy.

🔗 *Make yours a heart of gold* 🔗

*It is possible to take a stand for what you believe in,
you may be ahead of everyone, hopefully they will catch up.*

—singer Raffi

In Chapter 14 you built nerves of steel. Now it's time to build a heart of gold.

Irene Gut Opdyke was a heroine. As a young Polish girl under Nazi occupation, she smuggled terrified Jews to safety right under the nose of German officials. She even became the unwilling mistress of a German Major to save the lives of some Jews she was hiding in his basement.

During the Nazi era, it was so easy to follow the path of least resistance, to simply avert one's eyes. Doing nothing is usually the path of least resistance. But few people are happy doing nothing. Eventually, one looks back at a life of couldov beans. One thinks, "I wonder what I could have achieved if only I had tried."

Yet so often fear paralyzes us. Fear of making a mistake. Fear of what others might think. Or, in the case of Nazi Germany, fear of what soldiers might do. Irene didn't let fear paralyze her. Defiantly, she started helping the Jews, one little bit at a time. One day, a simple gesture of love, smuggling food to some, led to much greater acts of heroism.

Who needs help?

· The hungry
· The homeless
· The sick
· The animals
· The grievers
· The abused
· The planet

Because Irene Gut Opdyke dared to do it, she contentedly says, "I know that God touched my life." She moved her stones.

She was grateful because she did something good. Her story is not uncommon. Generous people tend to be more thankful than selfish people. And since gratitude is a key habit for maximum happiness (remember Chapter 9?), generous people are happier than selfish people.

After vandals smashed a statue outside a New York City church, a restorer volunteered to repair it. Returning the renewed statue to the church, the volunteer thanked the priest for letting him help. "That's the way it is with people who are generous," Father Bolduc explains. "They are the ones who say thank you."

You might have heard a popular story about the two terminally ill women who shared a hospital room. Every day, the woman near the window would describe the goings on, the weather, the children playing in the park across the street, the comings and goings. One day, the woman by the window dies.

The other woman, now alone, tells the nurse, "I miss my friend. She was always so cheerful. Most of all, I miss her descriptions of the weather and the park and all the comings and goings." The nurse looks puzzled, "You can't see any park from this window, just the roof of the hospital cafeteria. Besides, your roommate was blind." Blind with the eyes, yes, and having every reason to feel bitter. But generous of spirit, and no doubt she created as much joy in her own heart as in her room-mate's, when she described the imaginary scene out the window.

Another way to do good is to volunteer. Help needy children or families. Help disabled or sick people by volunteering at a hospital or community center. Work for a worthy cause—for human rights, for a rehabilitated environment, for safer streets.

You can help others improve themselves through professional associations. "All of us have employment on the side," jokes Jennifer Evans, a Webgrrls® leader. When I look at all the time I spend with Toastmasters, helping local clubs organize themselves and coaching newer members, sometime I wonder if that's not my full-time job.

Do good. Help others. Build a heart of gold.

Do-gooder magnetism

One filled with joy preaches without preaching.

—Mother Teresa

Do-gooders are attractive to members of the opposite sex. Here are two good reasons why. (Single readers, take notes.)

The first reason is obvious. The hand that feeds, that nurtures, that cradles, is unlikely to be the hand that strikes. Lets' face it, would you rather live with a partner who is generous and shares, or would you rather live with a partner that throws things and hits you?

A generous person is more likely to share both the benefits and the chores of marriage. She's more likely to be a good role model for their children. She's more likely to care and sympathize and support.

The second reason is that do-gooders are happier, as we've just seen. Of course, who wants to be around the grumpy person who selfishly avoids all happiness? Nobody, that's who. We would all rather be around people who laugh and smile (and stand up straight and nod and clap) and lift our spirits.

POP QUIZ:

What do selfish people use for birth control?

ANSWER: Their personalities.

How do you find a do-gooder partner? If you've been dating for a while, you've probably found yourself saying, "I'm tired of the bar scene." And who wouldn't be? If you hang out in bars, you meet the kind of people who, well, hang out in bars. After a while, that gets almost as fulfilling as taking a census of the worms in the garden. Actually, helping keep a dark, loud, smoky place from looking empty, night after night, hoping that somebody worthwhile will bring meaning to your life, is downright depressing. Remember—only *you* can make yourself happy.

If you want to meet someone who gives, why not go where people give? That's the idea behind volunteer singles networks springing up across the country. In Washington, D.C., they expected a couple hundred people to sign up. Instead, they got 4,000 members. As one organizer puts it, "It's much better to meet people up to their knees in mud than on a bar stool." And if you meet someone while volunteering for a worthy cause, what do you share in common? A worthy cause, of course, is better than a fetish for dark, loud, smoky places.

Generous people are more attractive because they are happy. Just taking that step and becoming a volunteer makes a person happier and, therefore, more attractive. Volunteering also makes a person more interesting, because it gives him something important to talk about.

Bray Goat and Sarah Sheep pop their heads over the rim of the well. For the first time, Farmer Brown notices that they are still alive. But that's impossible, he thinks. He must be seeing ghosts. Yikes! He hightails it for the hills.

The goat and the sheep exchange glances. All this time, they've been helping each other Climb their Stairways to Heaven. And as they help each other, they help themselves. Now they just have to jump up over the rim and enjoy the Green Pastures of Cloud Nine.

All through this chapter, I talk mostly about how you can feel happier by doing good. I don't talk about saving lives and fighting poverty. I don't talk about the need for shelters or the destitution in Third World countries. I could, of course, but I'm not here to preach.

A West Los Angeles school administrator explains the idea behind community service programs: "The point is not to make people feel bad about having so much, but good about sharing it with others."

This book was written with the same intent. It's about happiness, not about guilt. It's about lifting spirits, not grinding them down. You don't need to feel guilty to do good. Reject martyrdom. After all, if you make yourself miserable while making someone else happy…just how is the world better off? Feel great doing good. Whether by sharing a smile, or bringing food to shut-ins, you've got to spread the joy if you want to hold on to it. And you've got to hold on to it if you want to spread it.

Conclusion

ENJOYING HAPPINESS

CHAPTER 19

The view from the top step

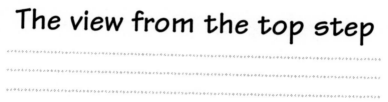

*There are many paths to the top of the mountain,
but the view is always the same.*

—Chinese proverb

One of the inspirations for this book was a story I received by e-mail a few years ago. The story is called *You Have Two Choices*. It's about Gerry, a man so full of zest for life that when someone asks, "How are you?" he responds, "If I felt any better, I'd be twins!" Good day, bad day, evening, morning, whenever the time, whatever the situation, Gerry wears a wide grin. One day, he leaves the back door of his restaurant unlocked. Bad move; he gets robbed and is left in a pool of blood.

As Gerry rolls into the hospital, he sees the horror and resignation in the eyes of the nurses and doctors. "Are you allergic to anything?" a nurse calls out. "Yes," Gerry responds. Everything stops. The doctors and nurses all wait to hear what Gerry's allergic to. Finally, he says, "Bullets!" The medical staff burst into laughter, and Gerry starts his lecture, "Look, I'm still alive, and I plan to stay that way. I saw the look in your eyes. Please operate on me as if I am still alive, not as if I am already dead. I'm in a great mood. Let's do it."

In the recovery room, back at work, and in the days and months ahead, Gerry continues to smile. A friend once asked Gerry how he could always be so cheerful. He answered, "There's plenty to feel good about and plenty to feel bad about. I have two choices. I simply choose to feel good. It's the one thing nobody can take from me."

That story so inspired me that I began referring to it every time Chantal was feeling upset about something. When office politics would place pressure on her, I would say, "You have two choices." When family or friends would do things that seem frustrating, I would say, "You have two choices." Before too long, she was saying this to me, too.

⚭ Make the choice ⚭

Your silver shoes will carry you over the desert.
If you had known their power, you could have gone back to your
Aunt Em the very first day you came to this country.

—Glinda the Good Witch to Dorothy in *The Wizard of Oz*

The research for this book kept me many hours at the library. One day while Chantal and I were there, a woman sat down at the next table. Her young girl, about five years old, started making a noticeable amount of noise. At first, this bothered Chantal. After a while, she noticed that the girl kept trying to wrestle the pen away from her obviously very patient mother. So Chantal went over to the other table and offered the little girl her pen and some paper.

By the time the library closed, Chantal and the little girl were drawing flowers and playing tic tac toe—and the girl's mother was accomplishing more reading, note-taking, and photocopying.

Chantal could have grumbled, complained, or brooded about the disturbance the girl was making. Instead, she made the choice to enjoy the girl's presence. That afternoon, Chantal made three people's lives happier. She moved her stones.

POP QUIZ: ....
What do you think of when you hear sirens?
ANSWER: Next time you hear sirens, instead of thinking, "Someone's in trouble," think, "Someone's rushing to the rescue." Ironically, as I sit in the middle of the Toronto hospital district typing this sentence, I hear the sound of someone charging to the rescue right now.

You control your happiness. It really is your choice. So why choose misery, when happiness is so much more pleasing? Why relinquish our right to choose happiness, when we can retain control over our attitude? Let's embrace what Viktor Frankl called "the last of the human freedoms—to choose one's attitude in any given set of circumstances."

You choose. You can build your Stairway to Heaven. You can climb that Stairway. And you can savor the glorious view from atop your Stairway, from the Green Pastures of Cloud Nine. But first, you have to choose. You've made the first choice—you've read the book. Now, will you apply the habits?

Apply the nine habits

*We should not let our fears
hold us back from pursuing our hopes.*

—President John F. Kennedy

Reading a book is easy. Changing your life takes more effort. These nine habits are easy to understand and easy to apply. But that does not mean they require no effort. You have to take steps to apply the habits.

To summarize, those habits are:

• **Throw a parade in your honor.** If you don't cheer for your great deeds, who will? And if you don't cheer for your other deeds, it's just too easy to forget how great they really are. By cheering every little success, rather than focusing on every little setback, we make happiness.

- **Distinguish yourself.** We're all the same, only different. It's what's different that makes you special. By feeling proud of our differences, rather than ashamed, we make happiness.
- **Count your blessings.** Life itself is a miracle, and it is simply crammed with wonders. By constantly saying thank you for everything we enjoy, rather than taking them for granted, we make happiness.
- **Learn, then burn.** Life gives us so many lessons, so many opportunities to learn. Somehow, we react to these lessons with frustration, anger, guilt, embarrassment. By learning the lessons, then burning the painful feelings, we make happiness.
- *Carpe diem.* There is so much to accomplish, so much to explore, so much to try. But fear sometimes holds us back, and, sooner or later, we regret all the things we were afraid to do. By seizing the day and breaking out of our Comfort Zone, we make happiness.
- **Slow it down.** The pace of life in the modern world builds up our stress level. By taking time to breathe, to relax, to be, we make happiness.
- **Pump it up.** Sometimes we react to stress by tuning out. We fail to keep our bodies in good shape, we donate our hours to the Merchants of Misery in TV-land, we waste away. By getting up and moving, we make happiness.
- **Choose YouBet people.** We are each a product of our environments, so make your environment the happiest possible. By surrounding ourselves with happy, positive, supportive, enthusiastic people, we make happiness.
- **Spread the joy.** When it comes to happiness, it is in giving that we receive. By sharing our joy with others, by raising the happiness in our environment, we make happiness.

Here are a few ideas to make the task easier, or at least increase the likelihood that you will succeed.

I suggest you write down the habits and place them somewhere you will see them every day, perhaps first thing in the day, perhaps at every change of situation. Next to your alarm clock is good. On the fridge could work. How about in your car, where you can see them just before getting to work and just before getting home? This technique worked for me when I used to commute.

Another method that works for me, as you have already read, is to share them with somebody close and enlist that person's help. You can support each other and remind each other of your mutual goals.

You can also share them with the world, as I am doing by writing this book. Let people know about the nine habits of maximum happiness.

Or how about making it a family project? You can work on one at a time. One month, each family member can take turns saying grace at the table. And you can make it a family project to say thank you at every possible opportunity. Another month, you could focus on noticing every little accomplishment each family member makes. What a fun way to grow together.

∞ *On top of the world* ∞

I finally found out the only reason to be alive is to enjoy it.

—U.S. novelist Rita Mae Brown

There might be no sage elder atop a mountain waiting just for you to ask, "Master, what is the secret to happiness?" But that's okay, because you can build your own Stairway to Heaven and climb over the Great Wall of Misery.

Life is wonderful on top of the Wall. You can see the Green Pastures of Cloud Nine. You can feel the warm breeze and hear the songs of the birds. You've made the effort to rise above it all…to build your Stairway to Heaven. Now you can bask in your habitat of maximum happiness.

Of course, life is a journey, not a destination. So don't slip back into bad habits. Make happiness a habit so that you remain on top of the Wall.

Bray Goat and Sarah Sheep are fortunate. There's not much chance of them falling back into the well—not now that it's filled with stones. But they've made up their minds to keep a safe distance from any other well or suspicious hole in the ground. They have no intention of falling back down. They built their Stairway, they climbed their Stairway, and they plan to stay right up here on the green pastures (which taste delicious, by the way).

Make yours a happy life.

Lightning Source UK Ltd.
Milton Keynes UK
27 April 2010

153445UK00001B/48/A

9 780595 178261